The Pre-histo
'The Midsummer Marriage'

The Pre-history of 'The Midsummer Marriage' examines the early collaborative phase (1943 to 1946) in the making of Michael Tippett's first mature opera and charts the developments that grew out of that phase.

Drawing on a fascinating group of Tippett's sketchbooks and a lengthy sequence of his letters to Douglas Newton, it helps construct a narrative of the Tippett-Newton collaboration and provides insights into the devising of the opera's plot, both in that early phase and in the phase from 1946 onwards when Tippett went on with the project alone.

The book asks: who was Newton, and what kind of collaboration did he have—then cease to have— with Tippett?

What were the origins of and shaping factors behind the original scenario and libretto-drafts?

How far did the narrative and controlling concepts of *Midsummer Marriage* in its final form tally with—and how far did they move away from—those that had been set up in the years of the two men's collaboration, the 'pre-historic' years?

The book will be of particular interest to scholars and researchers in opera studies and twentieth-century music.

Roger Savage is an Honorary Fellow in English Literature at the University of Edinburgh, UK. He is also the author of *Masques, Mayings and Music-Dramas: Vaughan Williams and the Early Twentieth-Century Stage* (2014).

Royal Musical Association Monographs
Series Editor: Simon P. Keefe

This series was originally supported by funds made available to the Royal Musical Association from the estate of Thurston Dart, former King Edward Professor of Music at the University of London. The editorial board is the Publications Committee of the Association.

29 Towards a Harmonic Grammar of Grieg's Late Piano Music
Benedict Taylor

30 The Genesis and Development of an English Organ Sonata
Iain Quinn

31 The Regulation and Reform of Music Criticism in Nineteenth-Century England
Paul Watt

32 Upper-Voice Structures and Compositional Process in the Ars Nova Motet
Anna Zayaruznaya

33 The Cyclic Mass
Anglo-Continental Exchange in the Fifteenth Century
James Cook

34 The Pre-history of 'The Midsummer Marriage'
Narratives and Speculations
Roger Savage

For more information about this series, please visit: www.routledge.com/music/series/RMA

The Pre-history of 'The Midsummer Marriage'

Narratives and Speculations

Roger Savage

LONDON AND NEW YORK

First published 2020 by Routledge

2 Park Square, Milton Park, Abingdon, Oxon, OX14 4RN
605 Third Avenue, New York, NY 10017

Routledge is an imprint of the Taylor & Francis Group, an informa business

First issued in paperback 2020

British Library Cataloguing-in-Publication Data
A catalogue record for this book is available from the British Library

Library of Congress Cataloging-in-Publication Data
A catalog record has been requested for this book

ISBN: 978-0-367-24316-6 (hbk)
ISBN: 978-0-367-78782-0 (pbk)

Typeset in Times New Roman
by codeMantra

Contents

Illustrations

Reproductions of Plates 3.1–8.2 by permission of the National Library of Scotland

Preface and acknowledgements

In a sketchbook of Michael Tippett's there is a draft, dating from around 1944, for the title-page of a libretto. It reads, 'Douglas Newton / An Opera / in 2 Acts / AURORA CONSURGENS / or The Laughing Children / MICHAEL TIPPETT'. A decade later, a vocal score was published with a title-page that ran, 'The Midsummer Marriage / An opera in three acts / Words and Music / by / Michael Tippett'. The works that these title-pages introduced were—and were not—one and the same, and my concern in what follows is with looking into this paradox and at the roles of the people involved in it. Who, to begin with, was Douglas Newton? What sort of collaboration did he have, then cease to have, with Tippett *en route* to the completion of *The Midsummer Marriage*? What were the origins of and shaping factors behind the work's original scenario and libretto-drafts? How far, after the spring of 1946 (when Newton withdrew from the project, and Tippett began in earnest to write music for it), did its narrative line and controlling concepts tally with, and how far did they move away from, those that had been set up in the years—the 'pre-historic' years, as I call them—of the two men's collaboration?

In looking at these issues, I have found myself concerned almost entirely with ideas, words, plot-devices and stage-situations, for although the composer had the sounds of possible music for the piece running through his head before 1946 as well as after it, he very rarely alluded to them in his writings at the time. It was plotting and texting that Tippett was concerned with when he put pen to paper in the mid- to late 1940s, especially in a sequence of six sketchbooks and a lengthy series of letters to Newton. The sketchbooks and letters are currently housed in the British Library (BL), and I make extensive use of them here. Between them, they help construct a narrative of the Tippett-Newton collaboration and throw light on the creation of the opera's own narrative and its plot, both in the collaborative phase and in the phase afterwards when the composer was going it alone as his own librettist. Hence the 'narratives' in my title. The 'speculations' are called for because there are lacunae in the documentation that occasionally need to be filled in some way. I've been explicit, I think, where I attempt to do this; responsible too, I hope.

Perhaps I should add that the approach to *The Midsummer Marriage* in what follows differs in kind from much that has been written illuminatingly and informatively about it since its 1955 premiere by such admirers as David Cairns, Robert Donington, Richard Elfyn Jones, Meirion Bowen, David Clarke and my near namesake Robert Savage. Quite properly, these writers have focussed almost wholly on the opera as an achieved thing: an opus complete in itself, to be considered either purely in isolation or in connection with other completed works. My concern, rather, is primarily with process: with the relationships, bold designs, happy accidents and sudden brainwaves that, on a conceptual-verbal level, brought that final achieved form about. So, in a sense what I write could be seen as something of a supplement to writings on Tippett that appeared *circa* 1980: the grand foundational treatment of the opera in Ian Kemp's *Tippett: The Composer and His Music*, Eric Walter White's 'I-was-there' chronicle of the last phase of its plot-development and John Lloyd Davies's detailed commentary on the libretto's sources and analogues. Not that my piece could have been written at that time: it would be another 15 years before the Tippett sketchbooks and his letters to Newton came to lie snugly in the BL, not too far from each other and ready for linked investigation. As it happens, little use was made of the material for several years after that, with the notable exception of Thomas Schuttenhelm's editing some of the letters for his 2005 *Selected Letters of Michael Tippett*. However, in the last five years or so there has been pleasing evidence that the letters to Newton have been gaining some attention. My concern here is with giving them more and bringing the sketchbooks out into the arena as well.

Appendix III comprises an inventory of *Midsummer Marriage*-related material in the six sketchbooks (British Library Add. MSS 72054-9). Reference to the letters to Newton in the notes (where Tippett is 'MT') is made as follows. At the BL these letters are assembled in two separately paginated scrapbook-type volumes: MS Mus 291 and MS Mus 292. In my notes I refer to these as BL291 and BL292, giving volume number plus the page number within the volume—e.g. 'BL291.146'—and adding a date, if possible, as precisely *as* possible, though this may sometimes not be very precise since Tippett rarely dated his letters to Newton. On the assigning of dates, for almost all my citations I have followed those ingeniously supplied *per* post-marks, paper-types, internal reference, etc. by BL staff when the Library acquired the letters in 1996, though I have sometimes adopted revisions of them suggested by Schuttenhelm when he was editing the ones he chose to include in his *Selected Letters*. (Where I have demurred from both the BL and Schuttenhelm over a particular dating, I have generally drawn attention in a note.) A little over a third of the passages I quote from the letters to Newton appear in *Selected Letters*, and when they do I have added the Schuttenhelm page-reference with the prefix 'Sch': e.g. 'BL291.146 (21 Oct 1943): Sch 158'. On the few occasions when my reading of Tippett's handwriting differs from Schuttenhalm's in a passage quoted, I print my own reading and put an asterisk (* = *sic*) against the 'Sch' page-number. Like Schuttenhelm, I silently expand Tippett's ampersands and his occasional abbreviated spellings ('wh' for 'which' and the like).

The author and the Royal Musical Association are grateful to the Michael Tippett Music Foundation and the Will Trustees of the Tippett Estate for kind permission to quote from the notebooks and letters of Michael Tippett, and also to the Douglas Newton Archive in New York for kind permission to quote from Newton MSS and transcribe poems of his (see Appendix I). For welcome help of various kinds in the writing of this piece, I am grateful to Nicolas Bell, Michael Burden, Patrick Carnegy, Owen Dudley Edwards, Richard Layard, Martina Maher, Gwyn Rhydderch, Virginia-Lee Webb — and, above all, to Oliver Soden.

R.S. December 2018

1 Michael Tippett and Douglas Newton to 1943

'Michael Tippett, *The Midsummer Marriage*, 1946–52: Opera in Three Acts; Libretto by the Composer; Première, Covent Garden, 1955.' Thus far the reference books, to a large extent correctly. *The Midsummer Marriage*'s music and the final version of its libretto were indeed Tippett's very own work, and the score was almost wholly composed between 1946 and 1952; so, it is not surprising that for a quarter of a century at least after its completion those dates and the attribution of the text to Tippett alone held sway; for example, in the illuminating chapter on the work in Eric Walter White's *Tippett and His Operas* of 1979. However, in an interview with Patrick Carnegy two years earlier, the composer had hinted that the project in fact stretched back further than 1946 and that back then he'd had in mind a collaboration on its text. 'I did try to find a librettist who could accept the material,' he said, 'but it did not work.' Ian Kemp's major 1984 study, *Tippett: The Composer and His Music*, went a little further, suggesting that Tippett had been mulling over the plot of *The Midsummer Marriage* since 1941 and revealing that a librettist-collaborator had actually been found in those early days. 'In fact he did try to work with one,' Kemp wrote, but it was to no avail. The 'one' was a certain Douglas Newton, though his name, presumably because it was not well-known in British operatic circles, was buried in a brief end-note rather than appearing in Kemp's main text. Seven years after Kemp, the two paragraphs on the opera's origins in Tippett's autobiography, *Those Twentieth Century Blues*, confirmed the germination-gestation period—the opera's 'pre-history', so to speak—and Newton's involvement in it.[1] The *Selected Letters of Michael Tippett* edited by Thomas Schuttenhelm

1 E. W. White, *Tippett and His Operas* (London, 1979 [hereafter '*Tippett*']), Ch. 3. P. Carnegy: 'The Composer as Librettist', *Times Literary Supplement* (8 July 1977), 834–5. I. Kemp, *Tippett: The Composer and His Music* (London, 1984), 213 and 491. Tippett, *Those Twentieth Century Blues* (London, 1991) [hereafter '*C20 Blues*']), 215–6; cf. M. Bowen, 'Introduction', in N. John, ed., *The Operas of Michael Tippett* (London, 1985), 7–17, p. 14.

that appeared in 2005 confirmed this. Schuttenhelm makes space for almost 60 letters to Newton, transcribed complete or in lengthy extracts from the sequence in the Tippett Archive at the British Library, including about a dozen that touch on the theatre piece that would become *The Midsummer Marriage*. It is a generous tranche and, taken with letters in Schuttenhelm's volume to other close friends of Tippett's (Francesca Allinson and David Ayerst especially), it gives one a sense of the course of the personal relationship most closely connected with the *Marriage* and of the early development of the opera itself. Still, Schuttenhelm only has room for a third of the British Library's sequence of 180 letters from Tippett to Newton, letters to which Newton's replies seem to be wholly lost. (Sadly for us, Tippett was no hoarder of such things.) To get a fuller picture of the collaboration, to release Newton from that end-note and to let more light in on the *Marriage*'s pre-history, one needs to look at the complete sequence, placing it side by side with other writings by the collaborators, especially the half-dozen surviving notebooks of sketches by Tippett for the opera's scenario and libretto—part of what he called 'my collection of draft scripts'[2]—which are also in the British Library.

Image 1.1 Douglas Newton *circa* 1950, photographer unknown; © *the Douglas Newton Archive, New York.*

2 White, *Tippett*, 59.

As the developing closeness of the two men is the context of the work's early growth, it may be useful to chart that closeness here, beginning with an introduction to the younger partner. Douglas Newton was born Brean Leslie Douglas Newton on 22 September 1920, to British rubber-planter parents in what were then the Malay States. Bree, as his mother called him—to good friends in the 1940s and 1950s he would be Den or Denny—was a forward and intelligent child. 'Everything began', he recollected in an interview late in life,

> when I was taught to read through an edition of Lord Macaulay's *Lays of Ancient Rome* printed in London in 1881. [...] I was five years old and lived in Malaysia. The book's illustrations engendered in me a veritable fascination with the past.[3]

There is a lot of the Den-Newton-to-be in embryo there. He was to become a very bookish young person (and one with a remarkably retentive memory); he would write over 3 dozen poems in early manhood, around 20 of which were published; and he would have a strong sense of classical antiquity, maintaining a lifelong passion for visual arts that linked past and present — sculpture (classical, tribal and other) in particular.[4] Spending his infancy on the Malacca coast of Malaysia would also have its significance in several ways. For one thing, though he was European in upbringing and bound sooner or later to make the journey 'home', his colonial infancy placed him at the south-eastern tip of mainland Asia, close to the point from which the great Indonesia-to-Melanesia archipelago starts to reach out into the Pacific, and the archipelago—one island in it particularly—would in time become central to his life.[5]

In 1927, six or seven years of age and burdened with some intense, disturbing memories of the Malacca of his infancy, Newton travelled

3 L. Mattet, 'Entretien avec Douglas Newton', *Arts & Cultures*, 1 (2000), 19–30, p. 20. Almost all the information in print about Newton's boyhood and adolescence is to be found in the Mattet 'Entretien', though it should be supplemented with Newton's prose piece on his earliest years, 'Rebus: or The Poet's Education', *Botteghe Oscure*, 11 (1953), 141–51.

4 For Newton's poem 'Archaic Art', see Appendix I. (For details of his published poems and evidence for further poems written but not published, see Appendix II.)

5 The world of adult expat-Brits in the Malay States in the inter-War years is nicely evoked in a surviving letter from Newton's mother to her 'dearest Bree' in the 1940s, included with the Tippett-to-Newton letters at the British Library. 'Is there any chance of getting the tigerskin back? it is such a pity to let it disappear like this, sometimes I could cry, I did take care of it, and the old Sultan would be very upset.' BL292.189 (4 Nov 1942).

to England. He was to spend the next three decades there. He had some formal schooling in London up to the age of 15, but, as a later account put it, he 'never earned a university degree' and was 'largely self-educated'.[6] He educated himself well, reading voluminously, voraciously and creatively—an American writer who first met him in the 1940s would describe him as 'the best-read person I have ever known'—and before long mixing with young British poets of the post-Auden, New Apocalyptic/Neo-Romantic generation. However, his preferred world at the time was that of museums and galleries. Ancient Egyptian art was a teenage passion; then around 1936 contemporary English painting and sculpture took hold, the controversial work of Jacob Epstein especially (he relished the controversy).[7] Through Epstein he encountered the tribal sculpture of Africa: a boost to his lifelong interest in the tribal and archaic. 'In the years before the Second World War', he recalled later, 'I haunted the British Museum,' and to work *in* a museum became and remained 'the dream of my life' (or so he once claimed when being interviewed for a museum job). However, war broke out in September 1939; the BM was closed 'for the Duration' (as the phrase went at the time), and Newton was compelled to lay more emphasis for a while on the professional-writer and poet-in-the-making aspects of his career.[8]

It was quite possibly during the summer or autumn of 1939, when he was not far short of his 19th birthday, that he first encountered Michael Tippett, then nearly 35. (They had almost certainly met by the end of August that year.)[9] The two men had two important things in common.

6 Journey to England: CV in *Penguin New Writing*, 29 (1947), 6. 'Never earned…': E. Kjellgren, 'Returning to the Source: Michael C. Rockefeller, Douglas Newton, and the Arts of Oceania', *The Metropolitan Museum of Art Bulletin*, Summer 2014, 28–37, p. 33.

7 'Best-read person': M. L. Settle, ed. A. Freeman, *Learning to Fly: A Writer's Memoir* (New York, 2007), 152. Epstein and controversy: Mattet, 'Entretien', 20; Kjellgren, 'Returning to the Source', 33.

8 For another enthusiast's feelings at the Museum's closure, see P. James, ed., *Henry Moore on Sculpture* (London, 1966), 157.

9 The strong implication (though not assertion) in Newton's essay on MT—*Crescendo* 14 (March 1948), 6—is that they had met before August 31. Towards the end of the century, MT (see *C20 Blues*, 122) and M. Bowen (*Michael Tippett*, 2nd ed. (London, 1997), 28) imply that the first meeting was several weeks later; but Newton's nearer-the-time testimony seems more reliable. Bryan Fisher, a member of MT's inner circle since late 1935, notes in his unpublished memoir, 'An Adventure in Living' (private collection), that he, Fisher, had become friendly with Newton by 1938; so it is conceivable that MT had met Newton through him earlier than the summer of 1939. For MT's situation in these years (and for much else besides), see O. Soden, *Michael Tippett: The Biography* (London, 2019), Chs. 14–16.

First, both were musical, and so quite possibly introduced by mutual musical friends at a time when Tippett was doing freelance choral and orchestral conducting in and around London and beginning to make a name for himself as a composer. Second, by the time war was declared in September 1939, both were pacifists. They would both in due course register as Conscientious Objectors (Tippett in 1940, Newton in 1941), awaiting the tribunal meetings of the Ministry of Labour, which would decide the form their exemption from military service would take; and in the months leading *up* to the conflict they could well have met at some gathering of like-minded people. But whenever and wherever they met, the younger man impressed the older as showing signs of 'good breeding and a live mind'.[10] Tippett was also impressed by Newton's gentleness, which, like his pacifism, was arguably part of a recoil from the casual cruelty, violence, bloodletting and indifference to suffering and death that he had observed on the Malacca coast in very early boyhood: cruelties he would later evoke vividly in a prose piece that he published in 1953, 'Rebus: or The Poet's Education'.[11]

Around the time War was declared, Tippett was beginning to set the libretto he had himself written for his oratorio *A Child of Our Time*. The text at that point wasn't finalised, and when it was it would need printing. Newton soon found himself helping out in both these areas: reacting to and advising on various small rewritings—(was 'telescope' a settable word? Tippett asked him; was 'sweetheart' too slangy?)—typing the text, getting estimates from printers, looking at proofs and so on. It was a process that would stretch out over several years and merge with Newton's coming to be appreciated in Tippett's circle as something of a Jack-of-all-high-cultural-trades: typographer, calligrapher, translator.[12] One of the earliest Tippett-Newton letters that

10 BL292.13 (7 June 1944).

11 Gentleness: see nn. 25 and 141 below. 'Rebus': as in n. 3 above. ('If anyone wants to know anything about the real psychic impact of what much of my life as a child in Malacca was like, he should read ['Rebus']. [...] There you have it undiluted, raw, and without context.' Newton, unpublished 'Autobiographical Notes'. This quotation from the 'Notes' and that at n. 226 are by kind permission of The Douglas Newton Archive, © 2017 Virginia-Lee Webb PhD. All Rights Reserved.

12 Printing etc.: e.g. *C20 Blues*, 136; BL291.33 (11 Nov 1941): Sch 141–2. MT himself sought Newton's advice for the cover of his anthem *Plebs Angelica* 'because of your eye for letter spacing' (BL291.221 [16 April 1944]); MT's colleague Walter Bergmann hoped that Newton could be persuaded in connection with a Morley College concert 'to translate the Latin Purcell duet instanter et celeritandus' (BL292.148 [4 Dec 1945]); and Francesca Allinson wondered if he might be interested in copying out the musical illustrations—a considerable number of them—for a book of hers 'in a classy writing for photographing' (BL292.186).

can be exactly dated was posted on 23 November 1939; it mentions three points in the final-draft libretto where verbal changes might be needed, reports that 'the music is pouring out', suggests a meeting at Morley College for Working Men and Women, a London base of his at the time—giving Newton directions how to get there as it would be his first visit—and adds, 'I've thought of the most surrealist plot for a play or an opera.'[13] Ten weeks later, the composer would write to his friend and colleague Alan Bush: 'I am reaching out towards opera — some years ahead';[14] but after that November letter he keeps silent for several years in his correspondence with Newton about ideas for operas or other music-theatre pieces (though the two men may of course have had some *viva voce* conversation about them).

No opera in the early letters then; but there were other things to write about. The *Child* oratorio continued to preoccupy. Did it, Tippett asked Newton in October 1941, need paring down? 'In this wildly destructive period, artistic proportion perhaps has to be tougher and deeper — à la Eliot — and that's the labours of Sisyphus.'[15] Then there was the 'Conchie' status the two men would come to share in the early War years, involving continued encounters with like-minded people and anxious feelings about their up-coming tribunals: in Tippett's case coming up in 1942, in Newton's in 1943. (When the tribunals eventually came about, both men declined to comply with the conditions laid down, for which Tippett famously served a London prison sentence in Wormwood Scrubs and Newton, who 'decided to refuse Civil Defence training and take the consequences', may well have been threatened with one.)[16] In 1940 and later there was also the matter of Newton's bed, board and employ. Tippett was, comparatively speaking, settled: he had a small house in Surrey near Oxted and would soon be taking up the Music Directorship at Morley College; but he was much exercised on his friend's behalf. Should Newton get a wartime clerical job or a farmhand's? Farming won out, and for a while Newton worked at a Quaker-run smallholding in East Grinstead with which his and Tippett's close mutual friend Francesca Allinson had connections. It wasn't too far from the Tippett bungalow, and the older man proposed a scheme whereby the younger would sleep-over at the

13 BL291.12 (23 Nov 1939): Sch *140 in part. (For 'or an opera' Sch has 'or our opera' — a seductive reading but one to be resisted). The plot may well have been that for the projected *Man with the Seven Daughters*; see n. 46 and associated main-text below.

14 T. Schuttenhelm, ed., *Selected Letters of Michael Tippett* (London, 2005), 128.

15 BL291.23 (20 Aug 1941).

16 Tippett's case: Kemp, *Tippett*, 40–43. Newton's: *C20 Blues*, 124, 163, 166.

bungalow several nights of the week and cycle to the farm, just as later in the War he suggested that Newton, who was developing a taste for the farming life, should set up and tend a smallholding of his own next to a caravan they could share on the Allinson family's East Anglian estate; but nothing seems to have come of either plan.[17]

Still, the two managed to see each other quite often when Newton was at East Grinstead and later when he moved to Cambridgeshire. They would rendezvous at concerts at Morley: Tippett was forthcoming with complimentary tickets for these and also took to paying Newton's train fares (his medical bills too). They would take brief holidays together, Tippett filling letters beforehand with complicated travel arrangements. Newton would stay for the occasional week or weekend with Tippett in Surrey, often being asked before setting out to 'bring a tin of Household Milk if you can,' 'Bring sugar please — absolutely stuck' and the like. (These were years of severe food-rationing.) And when in the summer of 1941 he began a succession of farm-working jobs in Cambridgeshire which would last most of the War—joining 'lorry-loads of conchies' (Tippett's phrase) hedging, ditching and growing field upon field of sugar beet alongside Italian war-prisoners—Tippett would occasionally stay with him at his digs in Cambridge: a town all the more appealing to the composer in that he had contact with such University folk as Edward Dent and Patrick Hadley.[18]

Sequestered as he was quite often in deepest Surrey, Tippett would ask Newton to find books and journals for him as part of their ongoing conversation about literature: a conversation ranging over the latest essays of Edmund Wilson, the newest poems by Edith Sitwell—both men were occasional guests at her Sesame Club salon—and the reviews, as they came out, of Eliot's *Four Quartets*. (Tippett knew that if he dropped an allusion to *Prufrock* or *The Waste Land* into a letter to Newton, it would be recognised.)[19] Newton's digs themselves

17 Clerk or farmhand: BL291.19 (16 July 1940). The farm: Schuttenhelm, *Selected Letters*, 394. Early plan: BL291.17-18 (24 June 1940): Sch 141. Later plan: BL292.140–41 (3 Oct 1944). For the Tippett-Newton-Allinson connection, see H. Southworth, *Fresca: A Life in the Making* (Brighton and Eastbourne, 2017), esp. Pt. 5.

18 Paying for Newton: e.g. BL291.111 (31 Aug 1943): Sch 152; BL292.35 (1 July 1944): Sch 171. Food rationing: BL291.25 and BL291.81 (19 March 1943), cf. *C20 Blues*, 125, 179, 181–2. Lorry-loads: *C20 Blues*, 122.

19 Edmund Wilson: BL292.51 (20 Aug 1944). Edith Sitwell: BL292.128 (Aug 1943). Sesame Club: Amis, *Amiscellany* (London, 1985), 65. Eliot's *Quartets*: *C20 Blues*, 124; *Prufrock*: BL292.148 (4 Dec 1945); *Waste Land*: BL291. 126 (28 Sept 1943): Sch 156. For MT's well-populated literary hinterland, see S. Robinson, 'Introduction' to her *Michael Tippett: Music and Literature* (Aldershot, 2002), 1–19.

quite soon became very bookish ones. He had several addresses in or near Cambridge in his first months there, but by autumn 1942 he had moved into, and for two-and-a-half years would stay at, 86 Chesterton Road, which overlooks Midsummer Common and the River Cam downstream from the University. It was the home of the distinguished philosopher G. E. Moore, his wife and their children; but the Moores *père et mère* were away in America from 1940 to 1944, and it was their 20-something pacifist son Nicholas—'the ubiquitous Nick', copious Neo-Romantic poet, anthologist and editor—who was in charge of the house. (Newton seems to have had a semi-independent basement or attic flat there.) Nicholas was in the process of wooing and winning his Marxist-'deb' muse Priscilla Craig and was writing a long chain of poems inscribed to her. Though Tippett found these wrong-headedly uxorious, he was 'really delighted' by the enterprise and efficiency that Moore, his friend John Bayliss and Den Newton showed in editing and prevailing on the singular Reginald Ashley Caton of the Fortune Press to publish *The Fortune Anthology*, which came out in 1942 and featured new poetry and prose by several young British writers, a few older ones and such Americans as the editors thought should be better known in the UK. (After its publication, Moore and Newton would plan a sequel for Caton, their *Atlantic Anthology* of 1945, Tippett having written to Allinson in autumn 1943 that Newton's 'affairs with Fortune are flourishing [...]. Anyhow he's making his niche with American stuff alright.')[20]

Two poems by Newton himself, 'Songes and Sonettes' and 'A Face like the Sun'—seemingly the earliest of his to appear in print—were published by Moore in 1944 in the first number of his short-lived slim magazine *New Poetry*: a number which also included work from this side of the Atlantic by Lawrence Durrell (a poet Tippett the year before had considered setting), Ronald Bottrall, Ruthven Todd and Moore himself, and from the other by Paul Goodman and Howard Nemerov. Tippett pretty certainly approved of that too. On the whole he liked Newton's verse. The young poet was showing him new poems in manuscript or typescript by 1942, and on New Year's Day 1943 the older man gave his critical blessing:

20 Newton contributed a bumptious one-third of the first anthology's joint preface and an enthusiastic essay on the Sitwells: *Fortune Anthology* (London, 1942), 9, 69–74. 'The ubiquitous Nick': see D. Stanford, *Inside the Forties* (London, 1977), 39–43. MT on Moore: BL291.179 (9 Jan 1944); MT delighted with Newton's anthologising: BL291.113 (31 Aug 1943); MT's letter to Allinson, 16 Sept 1943 (private collection).

> I've liked your writings very much and wish you'd do a great deal more — but I'll have to wait I guess till [your] time can be more easily spared from direct social experience or forced labour. I want you to accumulate as much of yourself as you can during this long winter of war [but with] enough habitual expression to keep a thread of creation against the spring.

Direct social experience and forced labour: this chimes with a memory of wartime pacifist Cambridge preserved by the young American writer who considered Newton the best-read person she had ever met:

> In the evenings, the poets and the philosophers, working as conscientious objectors in the Cambridgeshire fields, gathered in the pubs. Muscular in their work, sad from alienation to the war, they talked in that split tone of the past or of the future.

Patrick Heron, the distinguished abstract painter-to-be, was one of their number for some months and became a good friend of Newton's; but Newton also had friendly, non-curricular connections with University people, writing trenchant and well-informed short critical pieces on cinema (Eisenstein, Pudovkin, Clair, Welles) for *The Cambridge Review*—Heron for one enjoyed them—and joining a circle centring on the 'at homes' of a lively Reader in Economic History from the London School of Economics (LSE), Lancelot Beales, and his wife Taff. The Beales had been evacuated from London along with the LSE itself, which was billeted 'For the Duration' on a Cambridge college, Peterhouse. Newton became a protégé of theirs: something which was later to have benign effects on his private life and his career.[21]

Meanwhile, he was happy to help keep the wolf from Tippett's door by collaborating over the preparation of the composer's first radio talk for the BBC, one on Stravinsky in January 1943: listening

21 Poems by Newton in *New Poetry*: see Appendix II below. Setting Durrell: BL291.120–21 (27 Sept 1943). 'Liked your writings': BL291.57 (1 Jan 1943). Pacifist Cambridge: M. L. Settle, *All the Brave Promises* (First University of S. Carolina ed.: Columbia SC, 1995), 103. See M. Gooding, *Patrick Heron* (London, 1994), 31, for Heron's Cambridgeshire farming 'forced labour'. (Some letters of Heron's to Newton are to be found in the Douglas Newton Archive, New York [Box 3].) For Newton's film reviews, see Appendix II below. For the Beales, see R. Dahrendorf, *LSE: A History of the London School of Economics* (Oxford, 1995), 347, and *Oxford Dictionary of National Biography*, *s.v.* 'Hugh Lancelot Beales, 1889–1988'.

with him to 78 rpm records of *Petrushka* and *Les Noces* and coaching him in microphone delivery. And he was watching Tippett's own *oeuvre* grow—the latter part of *A Child of Our Time*, the Handel Fantasia, the Second String Quartet and the revision of the First, the stirrings of what would eventually be called Symphony No. 1—and taking a special interest in the composer's verse-setting in the two madrigals he wrote for the choir at Morley College to texts by Gerard Manley Hopkins and Edward Thomas. Some years later, Newton would publish a searching essay on 'The Composer and the Music of Poetry'—an essay which he may well have drafted in 1943 or 1944—and at one point in it he is not at all happy with Tippett's treatment of a phrase ('dapple-dawn-drawn Falcon') in the Hopkins setting, 'The Windhover', though he acknowledges that such phrases may in fact be unsettable. Newton could be quite severe over matters of words-plus-music. When Tippett's biggest vocal piece in 1943, the setting of prose by W. H. Hudson in the cantata *Boyhood's End*, was premièred that June, the composer reported to Allinson that it 'was a great success at Morley on Sat. — in fact everyone seems to feel it's the best thing I've done except Den — who thinks it unvocal and a too impossible text!' However, this didn't inhibit Tippett from suggesting later that Den and he might work together on an anthem for Canterbury Cathedral, and on a possible companion piece to *Boyhood's End*:

> Got [your] poems today and have read them — and think them to be good — I like the first two of the ones I haven't seen — News Item and Bishop and Naturalist — v. much indeed. If I do have a go at another cantata for solo voice, we might try a collaboration, because News Item, for instance, is just the technique — of transition from statement to apostrophe, so to speak.[22]

22 BBC Stravinsky: BL291.49 (late 1942): Sch 146; BL291.71 (Dec 1942): Sch 147; BL291.57 (1 Jan 1943). 'The Composer and the Music of Poetry': *The Score* 1 (August, 1949), 13–20. (Though not published until 1949, the essay makes no reference to any music or verse that first appeared after 1945, and to only two pieces [Britten's *Peter Grimes* and Dylan Thomas's 'Fern Hill'] dating from after 1943, reference to the latter pair quite possibly being introduced during revision of the essay in 1945–49.) 'Dapple-dawn-drawn' and Hopkins-setting: 'The Composer and the Music of Poetry', 16, 19. Reporting to Allinson on *Boyhood's End*: Schuttenhelm, *Selected Letters*, 106. Canterbury anthem: envelope of BL291.130 (21 Oct 1943). Companion piece: BL291.123 (28 Sept 1943). 'Bishop and Naturalist': see Appendix I below; for 'News Item', see Appendix II.

When first pondering *Boyhood's End* some months before, Tippett—ironically, given what Newton's opinion of the piece would be when he heard it—had considered dedicating it to him. ('Dedications are always the more personal side of the thing for me; and have [...] lots to do with the private man.') In the event they decided against it—'We'll leave it be just yet'—partly because the cantata was so much a celebration of the natural world and Tippett didn't associate Newton with nature. Instead, they kept open the possibility of 'a later dedication on a more extensive work'.[23] Yet, as things turned out, that dedication never came, which is strange, since it would clearly have been a significant act of love on Tippett's part, like the dedications of extensive works earlier and later to the other most important young men in his life: Wilfred Franks, John Minchinton, Karl Hawker and Meirion Bowen. For Tippett certainly had come to love his 'Denlein', and for a while it seems that Denlein was happy that this was so.

The composer's friendly concern seems to have turned to deep affection by late 1941: a time when, as Tippett later put it to Allinson, Newton had a 'need for physical warmth' from him. For several months after that, they shared beds during their snatched times together in Surrey and Cambridge, though it seems without genital contact ('shar[ing] a bed with you without sharing anything else').[24] This involved a degree of restraint on Tippett's part, but it was something he was quite happy to exercise. As he put it in November 1941,

> I suppose for you and me there's a slight adjustment to be made because I am sensually more indulgent, or rather potentially so — and more extroverted if you like — and also I have lived longer thus. But it's an adjustment which isn't a problem to me at all really, having too much instinctive sympathy with your naturally reticent affection.[25] In any case, oddly enough, it's not my own sensual expression that I want or miss, but I wouldn't have you miss some experience for unreal inhibitory reasons.

By late the following year Newton's affection seems to have become less reticent and Tippett's eros less inhibited: helped by its being imbued with the confidence (won through his Jungian self-analysis after

23 BL291.46 (21 Oct 1942): Sch 145; BL291.50 (late 1942): Sch 147.

24 To Allinson: Schuttenhelm, *Selected Letters*, 113. Sharing-not-sharing: BL291.56 (23 Dec 1942): Sch 148.

25 Cf. 'the little Den—the unheroic, pacifist, escapist, anything you like—but with gentleness' (MT to Allinson, 1942: Schuttenhelm, *Selected Letters*, 85–6).

the affair with Wilfred Franks in the 1930s) that, if/when eros had to withdraw, there would be no traumatic after-effects:

> I've grown frightfully fond of you, but I think it's alright. By that I mean I [...] can move from friendship towards love without a catastrophic cut-off on the way back. [...] Of the danger of that dark sinister world that was around Wilf there is nothing — it's virginal and sensual at the same time and just the natural warmth that is love.[26]

Letters between December 1942 and autumn 1943 suggest a good, if singular and carefully tuned, erotic union:

> I always have need to say that I can be trusted and that there will be an immediate response the other way to any limits [set by you]. [...] It doesn't half seem odd that now [as I get older] comes for the first time a double union — of the day and the night. And just as I fear less in my own pleasures I joy in yours in the measure as you want. I can't see much point in stinting ourselves of anything we have for one another, whether spiritual or sensual. Nor I hope do you. [...] It *may* give you a certain different sort of satisfaction satisfying me so exactly. And this may be possible till the proper person you're looking for comes along. [...] Don't worry yourself (I don't think you do) about queerness or not. The acts of love aren't altered or disturbed really by that problem. To live any intimacy never precludes another at another time. [...] Many people remain dual to the end anyhow.[27]

Can we be confident that Newton too was content with all this? No one in the Tippett circle—not even the talkative John Amis, who knew both of them well and considered Newton 'a very loving person'—appears to have left any record at the time of the younger man's view of the matter, and Newton's own letters and postcards from these years (of which there were clearly quite a few, if not as many as Tippett would have liked) have vanished.[28] Still, although arguments from silence are risky things, one

26 Adjustment: BL291.33–4 (11 Nov 1941): Sch 142. Frightfully fond: BL291.55 (23 Dec 1942): Sch 147–8. For the 'world around Wilf', see *C20 Blues*, 57–62.

27 Any limits: BL291.56 (23 Dec 1942): Sch 148. Double union: BL291.113 (Aug–Sept 1943). Different sort of satisfaction: BL291.93–4 (May 1943): Sch 161.

28 'Very loving person': see Southworth, *Fresca*, 127. 'Send a post card if you can' and similar encouragements are quite frequent in MT's letters to Newton, and he wasn't alone in wanting to hear from him more often. Patrick Heron (see n. 21 above) would chaff his friend over his tardiness in replying to letters, and Newton's mother in her letter about the tigerskin (see n. 5 above) remarks that 'Once again

can reasonably hazard that Newton *was* content at the time, simply because (with the exception of the allusion to a 'very little storm in the tea cup' in October 1943)[29] there is nothing in Tippett's profuse correspondence to indicate that he was not, and Tippett, for all his powerful ego and artistic self-preoccupation, had come by the 1940s to have antennae sensitive towards the state of his friends' feelings and wouldn't have held his tongue in his letters to Newton if there were big emotional problems between them. Hindsight-judgement 50 years later confirms that there were not. Writing to Amis in the 1990s, Newton made it clear that he harboured no regrets over walking a little on the wild side with Tippett back in the 1940s. Amis's musical memoir of 1985, *Amiscellany*, had recalled, as part of its lively account of the Tippett circle, that

> before and after the time I knew Michael best, the friends who shared his double bed had had a touch of the delinquent about them, but during my time, from about 1942 to 1946, the only delinquency about the poet Douglas Newton (Den), was that he was, like Michael, a conscientious objector, and that the authorities were playing cat and mouse with him.

Newton was in his late 60s and based in America by the time Amis's book caught up with him. It earned and retained his admiration, though when he wrote to Amis about it in November 1991 he roguishly affected to have been

> somewhat offended by bits of it. Not a jd [juvenile delinquent]? Was not getting into even an innocent bed with our old friend MT not a sign of a certain jd-ism? Surely so. Even though I can assure you it wasn't an erotic riot at any time. Respectful yes

— adding a month later:

> I always thought [...] that then [in the 1940s] I was hopelessly what's now called a wimp, and so perhaps a venture into an alternative life-style was perhaps mildly daringly a sign of breaking into a certain independence?

---

you seem to have dematerialised', signing off with 'Much love, write soon, and when I say write soon I mean write soon, and nothing else but.' MT was familiar with Newton's dematerialising, writing to Mary Lee Settle in 1945 or 1946 that he knew 'Den's habits [and was] used to them', and that 'never hearing from him by word or sign [...] was always his habit.' BL292.179.

29 BL291.137 (13 Oct 1943): Sch 156.

To make doubly sure that Amis didn't think he was genuinely offended, Newton stressed that Amis's remark about his not being a juvenile delinquent really hadn't annoyed him at all. Rather, 'I was just ironically wishing I had been less green and a bit wilder.'[30]

It was against these backgrounds—of a close if not wholly balanced relationship, of shared pacifist ideology, of real intellectual engagement—that collaboration on the piece we know as *The Midsummer Marriage: An Opera in Three Acts* began.[31]

30 Amis: *Amiscellany*, 171. Newton admiring the book: Newton to Amis, 30 November 1991 and 17 January 1996. 'Somewhat offended': Newton to Amis, 30 November 1991. 'I always thought': Newton to Amis, 31 December 1991. In other letters at this time Newton refers to MT as an 'old cobber' and notes with pleasure that MT is 'evidently happy' in his old age (17 May 1992; 11 April 1992). (The quotations from Newton's letters to Amis here and at nn. 225 and 226 below are by permission of The Douglas Newton Archive, © 2017 Virginia Lee-Webb, PhD. All Rights Reserved.)

31 MT included a detailed plot summary of the opera in its final 1952 form in one of his sketchbooks (see below, Appendix III: Fifth Sketchbook).

2 Plotting a masque

'Refashioning the Traditions'

Tippett had told Allinson in 1941, 1942 and early 1943 of the first stirrings and 'slowly maturing conception, [...] growing inside and out', of a piece that was to be a '*divina commedia* [...] in the true *Zauberflöte* tradition'.[32] It was only in the late summer of 1943, however, in the weeks following his release from imprisonment in Wormwood Scrubs for non-compliance with his Conscientious Objector registration, that the 'pre-historic' existence of *Midsummer Marriage* began to take on active collaborative life. Not that anyone knew the piece by that name at the time, or thought of it as an opera. Rather, it was an untitled Masque in Two Acts: 'masque' being a form Tippett would have known from his concert-going in the 1930s (Vaughan Williams, Lambert) and from his association with Morley College, where English music, from Dowland and Gibbons to Purcell, was much played and sung, so that seventeenth-century ideas of masquing would not be far away.[33] Tippett wrote to Newton late that September, following a meeting earlier in the month (their first after a separation of several weeks because of 'prison on my part and harvest on yours'), that 'the masque begins to move again, and I may have it down in embryo by the time you turn up.' Turn up, that's to say, to discuss it in detail, for it had been decided that the younger man was to help with the scenario and then to write the words for the alternating sung and spoken text of this '*Singspiel* not pure opera'.

32 Schuttenhelm, *Selected Letters*, 74, 94, 97.

33 'Masque' in the early 1940s could signify a variety of things, backward-looking and forward-looking. Rolf Gardiner, whose rural-communal-allegorical masques at Springhead MT may have known, caught the general mood when he urged in 1945 that 'the masque form, about which there is some eternal magic and rightness, needs cultivation in a number of experimental ways' (*New English Weekly* 28/4, 8 Nov 1945).

To the letter in which we've seen Tippett responding to a batch of poems Newton had shown him ('have read them — and think them to be good') he added significantly: 'It augurs well for the masque.' It was an endorsement of his Denlein that he repeated in a letter to Allinson several months later.[34] From then until the spring of 1946, he would think of Newton as the work's librettist.

The Masque was to be multimedia, many-levelled and essentially allegorical-symbolic. That autumn of 1943, Tippett wrote to Allinson that he was keeping before himself 'the Elizabethan ideal of various planes of acceptance: dramatic entertainment, spiritual drama, poetry etc., all in one'; in a letter to David Ayerst about the problem of finding effective symbols in a complex age, he explained that

> the masque will be an attempt to deal with this matter of the healing symbol, or symbol of healing — a symbol in this sense being something which cannot be plucked to pieces either intellectually or from sensibility and is by its nature a pleroma.[35] [...] [It will be] syncretistic of course, but leaning more to Apollo than Dionysus — or rather a fresh attempt to divide experience between them according to the needs of the dual flesh. Union is therefore part of the final symbol — but I hope it won't get too transcendental.

The time of healing union in the Masque, as in *Child of Our Time*, was to be spring. Writing to Newton in September 1943, Tippett says admiringly of Edith Sitwell's recently published 'Green Song' that

34 Meeting in early Sept: MT, letter to Allinson, 16 Sept 1943 (private collection). Several weeks' separation: BL291.114 (3 Sept 1943): Sch 153. 'Masque begins to move': BL291.118–9 (27 Sept 1943). *Singspiel*: Schuttenhelm, *Selected Letters*, 94. 'Augurs well' again: *C20 Blues*, 178.

35 *Pleroma* = a transcendental indivisible of cosmic forces in perfect interplay: a Biblical term adopted by the Gnostics and borrowed by Jung, MT's likely source for it. Jung, 'Sermo I' in *VII Sermones ad Mortuos*, tr. H. Baynes (London, 1925): 'the qualities of the pleroma [...] are pairs of opposites [...] such as fullness and emptiness, [...] good and evil, [...] the One and the Many'. Also see A. Storr, ed., *The Essential Jung: Selected Writings* (Princeton, 1983), 341–3. MT's definition of 'symbol' here is Jungian too; cf. Ch. 5 of Jung's *Psychological Types*: 'A symbol must be by its very nature un-assailable [...]; it must also be sufficiently remote from comprehension to resist all attempts of the critical intellect to break it down.' *Collected Works of C. G. Jung*, Vol. 6, tr. H. Baynes and R. Hull (London, 1971), 237. For the importance to MT of *Psychological Types*, see *C20 Blues*, 62, and D. Ayerst in I. Kemp, ed., *Michael Tippett: A Symposium on His Sixtieth Birthday* (London, 1965), 66.

it has 'a sound of *future* spring — somewhat as the oratorio has — while the masque is a *present* spring — or an eternal one, rather'.[36] By that time a broad sense of the basic plot along with a skeleton cast of characters for this piece of springtime symbolism was already in his mind. Tippett had told Allinson some months before that the work was 'straightening itself out, though it's very difficult to make neat transitions to the mythological material'. Now there was a lot to be done to realise the whole thing conceptually, theatrically and verbally before he could embody it musically — and Newton was to be his partner in the realising of 'our masque' (as Tippett would call it in a 1945 letter to him).[37]

We only have a couple of indications from Tippett as to how that basic plot and cast had come into being. One, in his late autobiography, is the rather hazy recollection of the contribution made to a linked group of early projects by an ancient Chinese text, the *I Ching* or *Book of Changes*: a book deeply revered as a source of oracular wisdom and divination in the East.

> The I Ching suggested various possibilities, at that time [= *ca* 1939], for the masque that was finally to become *The Midsummer Marriage*. [...] [It] evolved from a masque with the title, *The Man with Seven Daughters*, through various intermediary stages: in an early sketch it was called *Octett*, and consisted of the eight main trigrams from the I Ching, linking the seasons to the elements, to musical instruments etc.[38]

Tippett may well have had his *I Ching* initiation courtesy of another Chinese classic, one that he liked and tried to get his friends to appreciate: the anonymous seventeenth-century Taoist treatise, *The Secret of the Golden Flower*. This had been put into German in the 1920s by Richard Wilhelm and thence into English in the 1930s by Cary Baynes, the English version being capped with a commentary

36 'Elizabethan ideal': Schuttenhelm, *Selected Letters*, 111. Cf. MT's description, in connection with his *Mask of Time* 40 years later, of 'the Renaissance masque, which was a theatrical form with a great diversity of ingredients, a mixture of formality and flexibility, with an ultimately lofty message': M. Bowen, ed., *Tippett on Music* (Oxford, 1995), 246. 'This matter of the healing symbol': Schuttenhelm, *Selected Letters*, *242. 'Green Song': BL291.119 (27 Sept 1943).

37 'Straightening itself out': Schuttenhelm, *Selected Letters*, 97. 'Our masque': BL292.128 (Aug 1945).

38 *C20 Blues*, 90 and 215. Back in the 1940s MT's name for the superseded masque-project was *The Man with the Seven Daughters* (Schuttenhelm, *Selected Letters*, 82).

by a friend of Wilhelm's and hero of Tippett's, Carl Gustav Jung. *The Secret* makes several references to the *I Ching*: references that are elucidated in Wilhelm's introduction and notes.[39] Then in the later 1930s Tippett met the renowned sinologist Arthur Waley, who could have expanded on *I Ching* backgrounds for him and who, at that time or soon afterwards, gave him a copy of Wilhelm's ground-breaking if idiosyncratic German version of the complete text, *I Ging: Das Buch der Wandlungen*[40] (also endorsed and promoted by Jung). Tippett's German was good enough to cope.

Through Wilhelm and Waley, Tippett learnt that the *I Ching*'s DNA, so to speak, was a set of eight three-line figures known as 'trigrams', each with its own wide-embracing name (*Li*, 'the clinging'; '*K'un*, 'the receptive', etc.). If one put two of these trigrams together, one made a 'hexagram': a significant yoking of concepts. If one put all eight of the trigrams into all their possible pairings (8 × 8), one generated the 64 hexagrams, each having its oracular text, that were fundamental to Chinese traditional wisdom. Late in life Tippett would turn to the 64 hexagrams,[41] but in the 1930s and 1940s it was 'the eight main trigrams' themselves that intrigued him. In ancient China they had attracted and been linked with several parallel listings of eight, and at one point or another in the Masque-project sketchbooks Tippett calls on five of these 'eightsomes': the eight points of the compass, elements of the landscape, products of the natural world, instruments of music and relationships in a family.[42] If we bring his chosen eightsomes together and set them out in what was known as the Inner World Arrangement, this octagon emerges:

39 Meaning a lot to MT: *C20 Blues*, 89. Material relevant to the *I Ching*: R. Wilhelm and C. Baynes, trs., *The Secret of the Golden Flower: A Chinese Book of Life* (London, 1931), 18–19, 55, 60, 69, 72–3.

40 *C20 Blues*, 89. When MT writes there that 'Waley was very dismissive of [the *I Ching*]: he said that it was mainly a collection of folk-sayings, just like "Red skies at night, shepherd's delight"', he half misrepresents, half accurately recalls Waley. Waley in fact had real respect for the ancient texts at the heart of the *I Ching* and sinologists have regretted that he didn't go on to make the translation/edition he seems to have contemplated. But he did use the 'Red skies at night' analogy when writing about them—see *Bulletin of the Museum of Far Eastern Antiquities*, 5 (1933), 121—and very likely used it in his table-talk too.

41 See n. 215 below, and Bowen, *Tippett on Music*, 254.

42 *I Ching* eightsomes in MT's sketchbooks: Add. MS 72054, 2r, 4r; 72058, 5v-18r. For Chinese listings of eight, see *The I Ching or Book of Changes: The Richard Wilhelm Translation*, tr. into English by C. Baynes, 3rd ed. (London, 1968), esp. pp. 268–79.

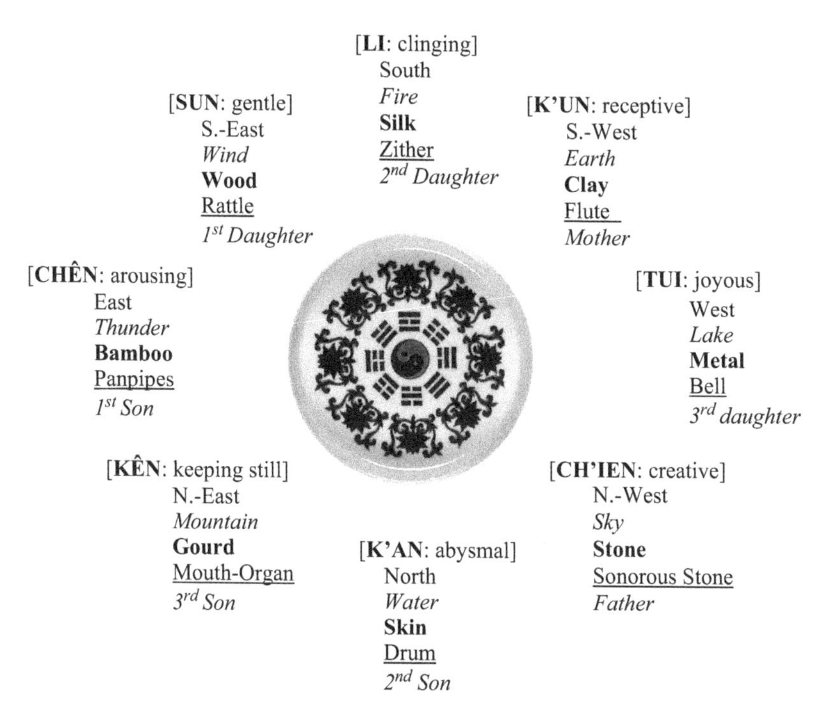

Image 2.1 Trigrams in the 'Inner World' arrangement and Yin-Yang symbol, Chinese porcelain saucer-dish, eighteenth century, Durham University Oriental Museum, DUROM 1969.229a; *reproduced by permission of Durham University Museums.*

Two projected, planned but unwritten works grew out of links Tippett made between these parallellisms: the one that he calls *Octett* in his autobiography, seemingly a cantata-like piece 'linking the seasons to the elements, to musical instruments etc' (Earth with Flutes, Wind with Rattles and so on);[43] the other a sequence of short

43 Wilhelm's *I Ching* text says little about musical instruments and has no eightsome of them, nor does his *Golden Flower*; but MT evidently had access to the Chou Dynasty's *Bayin/Pa-yin* ('eight-tone') system which links each of the *I Ching* trigrams to one of the eight earthly elements (boldface in the octagon above) and then links each element with one of an eightsome of instruments (such as those underlined in the octagon). He could have found accounts of the system in Victorian surveys such as J. Rowbotham's *History of Music* (1885), I. 286, and J. van Aalst's *Chinese Music* (1884, rep. 1933), 47 — or could have been personally instructed in it by his erudite, musically sophisticated friend Waley. For the *Bayin*, see W. Kaufman, *Musical References in the Chinese Classics* (Detroit, 1976), 157.

dramatic narratives that link family-position to climate and landscape (Thunder and the First Son, Wind and the First Daughter, etc.).[44] His notes for this latter indicate that he was paying close attention to the oracle-texts in the *I Ching*; they tantalise with characteristic quotations from Blake, Hölderlin and Yeats, and they hint at a few musical ideas (here 'chanting on a kind of ground', there 'a great cry sustained by organ pedal'); but they give us little idea of the artistic form the project as a whole was to take.[45]

The other work Tippett mentioned in old age in connection with the *I Ching*-fuelled evolution towards *The Midsummer Marriage* was *The Man with the Seven Daughters*. This was to have been a modern-dress farcical family-tale in masque form involving the severe drubbing meted out to a decayed paterfamilias by his children: a result of the mayhem following the surprise arrival of a dashing young stranger. As things turned out, this project wasn't carried through either. (Ideas for the spring-tide masque were pushing it aside: 'It does look', Tippett told Allinson early in the 1940s, 'as if the *Seven Daughters* will be stillborn, poor dears.')[46] But the *Seven Daughters*' planned focus on momentous change in an eight-character family suggests connections with the *I Ching*'s family of eight, though at the same time it connects cross-culturally with the ceremonial slayings of the Old Year Priest that James Frazer was adducing in his *Golden Bough*. (Tippett had been devouring Frazer whole in the late 1920s and 1930s.)[47] And if one is making cross-cultural links of this sort, it's relevant too that the family eightsome in the *I Ching*—a text dear to Jung—could be seen as an Eastern analogue to an eightsome in Jung's own *Psychological Types*: a text dear to Tippett which he had first encountered in the early 1930s and which, according to his friend David Ayerst, he 'read and re-read'. In the *Types*' second chapter—Tippett thought it 'brilliant'[48]—Jung posits four basic human responses to the world: a 'quaternity' of Thinking, Feeling, Sensation and Intuition. He insists, though, that the four are permeated by his celebrated Introvert – Extravert duality; so it's a matter of 4 × 2, which produces (as he puts

44 BL Add. MS 72058, 5v-18r.
45 But see Soden, *Michael Tippett*, 432–3, on MT's 1953–4 plans for a *Festival in the Humane City*.
46 Schuttenhelm, *Selected Letters*, 97; cf. 82–3.
47 Ayerst in Kemp, *Michael Tippett: A Symposium*, 66.
48 MT reading and re-reading Jung: Ayerst in Kemp, *Michael Tippett: A Symposium*, 66–7. Brilliant chapter: Schuttenhelm, *Selected Letters*, 257.

it in a related 1936 essay, 'Psychological Typology') 'a set of eight demonstrable function-types'. We might construct an *I Ching*-like octagon:

	Extraverted Thinking	
Introverted Intuition		Extraverted Feeling
Introverted Sensation	+	Extraverted Sensation
Introverted Feeling		Extraverted Intuition
	Introverted Thinking	

Jung was quick to say that it was 'not the purpose of a psychological typology to classify human beings into categories'. Tippett too could see that the approach risked being overly 'schematic', yet it had real attraction for him. He recalled that he

> discussed with Wilf and others which types we all were. The 'introverted intuition' type seemed to suit me quite well. The type farthest from me would be the 'extraverted sensation' type, and I decided this applied to Wilf.

It may also have struck him that some such *I Ching*-recalling Jungian schema could be used to underpin an allegorical or symbolist theatre-piece effectively.[49] An octet of characters or Types, not duplicating Jung's or the *I Ching*'s yet similarly structured and with elements of eros, class and the supernatural added in the manner of *A Midsummer Night's Dream* and *The Magic Flute*: such an octet would surely open up 'possibilities [...] for the masque that was finally to become *The Midsummer Marriage*'. It is tempting to speculate that Tippett hit on a structure like this:

49 Jung on Types: *Psychological Types*, 68 and 554 (cf. 482–3 and 523). MT on Types: *C20 Blues*, 62. As far as I know, Jung himself nowhere explicitly analogises his eightsome of Psychological Types with the eightsomes of the *I Ching*. However, he was concerned with both at the same time, later recalling that his intensive work on the Types in the early 1920s had been accompanied by a growing interest in Taoism: *Memories, Dreams, Reflections*, ed. A Jaffé (London, 1947), 233–4.

Sensual Young Man

Girl of Imagination — Worker-Boy

Sybilline Prophetess + Male Boss-Figure

Worker-Girl — Boy of Imagination

Idealistic Young Woman

Certainly some such octagon seems to have formed the skeleton *dramatis personae* of Tippett's Masque-project in September 1943, when he and Newton began collaboration on the work in earnest. The octagon-as-octagon would have had the blessing of Tippett's Jungian-analyst friend John Layard, who was writing in or around the same year that eight was 'the number signifying completion':

> The number 8 is a reduplication of 4, representing the 4-square earth, the 4 cardinal points, the 4 psychological functions and innumerable other quaternities of psychological and religious import. In dreams it is often represented by 4 couples — 4 men and 4 women.[50]

The other indication Tippett gave as to the origin of the Masque's plot lies in his recollection (in an essay that first appeared in the *Observer* newspaper in 1952) of a seminal image that had come to him ten-or-so years before:

> I *saw* a stage picture (as opposed to hearing a musical sound) of a wooded hilltop with a temple, where a warm and soft young man was being rebuffed by a cold and hard young woman (to my mind a very common present situation)[51] to such a degree that

50 Layard, *The Lady of the Hare* (London, 1944), 57–8. For MT in 1956 on connections between the number eight, the writings of Jung, contemporary Black African culture and the complete human being (comprising male + female + The Word), see his *Moving into Aquarius* (London, 1959), 111. (The original Jungian quaternity supplied the basis for two four-character conversation-pieces published in the 1940s and 1950s: Auden's *Age of Anxiety*, 1946, and the Priestley-Hawkes *Dragon's Mouth,* 1952.)

51 On gender-tension of this sort, MT writes to Newton that 'there is a lot of it in the Masque: because the shift towards the masculine by women has been epochal in consequences and is the devil to resolve. Men are *forced* to become subjective and

> the collective, magical archetypes take charge—Jung's *anima* and *animus*—the girl, inflated by the latter, rises through the stage-flies to heaven, and the man, overwhelmed by the former, descends through the stage-floor to hell. But it was clear they would soon return.[52]

One can see how a basic plot could emerge from combining that image with an eightsome of characters related *inter alia* to those of Jung and the *I Ching.* Four couples would be involved, with something of a special focus on the sensual young man and idealistic young woman whom Tippett had seen in his 'stage picture'. One might align that pair with the *K'an - Li* diagonal of the *I Ching* octagon. In the account of the trigrams in his introduction to *The Secret of the Golden Flower*, Richard Wilhelm connects *K'an* with Eros, Water and the Moon, and *Li* with Logos, Light and the Sun, declaring that 'the marriage of *K'an* and *Li* is the secret magical process which produces the child, the new man'. Tippett would later write to Newton imagining the pair having a momentous spat on the morning of what the young man had hoped would be their wedding day, and it's a clear case of Logos-Light-Sun *vs* Eros-Water-Moon:

> She says she is not in wedding dress because she needs to get away to *think* — he says, at same time — 'but why mountaineer costume?' She replies: 'I am driven to see the sunrise, to see the beginning of something new.' He: 'No — I prefer I'm sure the moon, on a bee-youtiful night, and with one's only love and the old, old story.' She: 'yes, you would of course!' And then [he] somehow twists it so that she might as easily see the dawn by going below to the sun at night in the sea — and she retorts he might as easily reach the moon by going for ever up the mountain.[53]

It's not certain how detailed the plot had become in Tippett's mind at the point of his release from Wormwood Scrubs. Certainly a vigorous confrontation between his *animus*- and *anima*-led lovers

---

to live in the normal female atmosphere of emotionality — but somehow the matter has to resolve at a deeper or higher (both) level.' BL291.182 (13 Jan 1944).

52 'The Birth of an Opera', in Bowen, *Tippett on Music*, 201.

53 *K'an* and *Li*: *Secret of the Golden Flower*, 19; cf. n. 177 *infra*. The spat: BL292.130 (19 Sept 1945).

and some related *Magic Flute*-like goings-on were there from the start, and letters to Allinson and Newton, mainly from late 1943 and early 1944, indicate that there was by that point a chorus of 'laughing children' deriving from the children in the shrubbery in T. S. Eliot's poem 'Burnt Norton', that a divination scene (by crossword-puzzle perhaps) was being considered, that the principal pair of lovers would be linked to a mysterious silent male dancer with an even more mysterious girl-friend and that there would be a quartet of other characters centring on the heavy father of one of the loving pair. He would be a businessman, attended by his personal fortune-teller, his secretary and his secretary's boy-friend. Knowing all this and glancing forward to the plot-sketches of a few months later, one can reasonably hazard that by September 1943 the narrative went something like this. A He- and a She-Ancient are presenting a masque rather in the manner of a Brechtian *Lehrstück* for a lively, articulate and much-amused bunch of their Neophytes, the Laughing Children (comprising a 'singing chorus' and a 'dancing chorus'). In the show, they and we see two young lovers, George and Margaret. They meet for a secret wedding, only for idealistic Margaret to call it off, rebuffing sensual George (who seems to have some sensuality to spare for a friend in the Neophyte audience, the mute dancer Strephon). As their controlling *anima* and *animus* take charge, George and Margaret set out quarrelsomely on complementary journeys, in his case to 'hell' then 'heaven', in hers to 'heaven' then 'hell'. During these, Margaret's father, the boss-man King Fisher, arrives on the scene, determined to rescue his child from the underworld, which is where he is convinced she has gone with George. To help him, King Fisher has his pretty secretary Bella and the brainy working-class boy Jack (he of all trades). Jack tries to retrieve Margaret, but the gates to the underworld are beyond his skills to open. So King Fisher calls on his clairvoyante. Enter Madame Sosostris. This veiled lady foretells what will come to pass, possibly in a scene of divination (with that crossword-puzzle maybe). Not being believed, she recommends that the King search for the truth himself in the depths of his own proper realm, the ocean. Wonders ensue, which draw Strephon and his Neophyte-dancer girl-friend into the action. They enrage King Fisher. Mightily provoked, he attempts to unveil Sosostris, at which she vanishes. A vision of the united George and Margaret appears in her place — a vision that fells the King. The lovers are returned to earthly actuality and, once Jack and Bella (now Doctor and Nurse) have brought King Fisher back to a feeble semblance of life, the two couples—George and Margaret, Jack and Bella—are married.[54]

With its supernatural stage-machinery to facilitate George and Margaret's ascents and descents; its wondrous props emerging from the kingdom of the sea; its foregrounded allegory of the sexes, classes and ages; and its climactic epiphany of united lovers followed by wedding celebrations, this was a plot that had the markings and makings of a true masque in the seventeenth-century English court tradition. Its stage-audience of Neophytes was part of that tradition too: explicit awareness of a show's spectators was central to traditional masquing. Further, court masques hadn't been afraid to be erudite and allusive, and the new Masque was just as bold. Its He- and She-Ancients are clearly relations of the pair in Part V of Bernard Shaw's *Back to Methuselah*. George and Margaret flaunt an *anima* and *animus* out of up-to-date Jungian psychology. The Egyptian Sosostris comes from Eliot's *Waste Land* and King Fisher from medieval Grail legends, very probably by way of the chapter on the Fisher King in Jessie Weston's *From Ritual to Romance*, a book made much of by Eliot in his *Waste Land* 'Notes'.[55] Strephon, in name at least, hails both from the tongue-in-cheek Arcadia of Gilbert and Sullivan's *Iolanthe* and from the fantasy future-time (also vaguely Ancient Greek) of Shaw's *Methuselah*. Jack's wearing the multiple hats of mechanic and doctor—later versions of the scenario will also have him as diver, plumber, fisherman, policeman, best man, technician and builder—aligns him with the Shape-Changer of various myth-sequences (also with the time-honoured Trickster at one point to come, when he masquerades as a magician). All the characters, Tippett was to

54 For the journeys of *animus* and *anima*, see the 'stage picture' above, n. 52. The Margaret-George-Strephon triangle, complete with names, is in place by the time of MT-to-Newton, BL291:147–8 (21 Oct 1943): Sch 159. Letters to Newton of early the following February (BL291.189–93: in part in Sch 165–7) suggest that the foursome of King Fisher, Sosostris, Jack and Bella was in existence several months before that date. For the scene of divination, see a letter of MT's to Allinson of spring 1943 (private collection): 'I've thought of a possible "divination" for the masque – by crossword. [...It] leads to much farce and punning, and there may be better methods.'

55 Mme Sosostris: see O. Soden, 'Madame Sosostris, Famous Clairvoyant(e)', in D. de Sousa, ed., *The Edinburgh Companion to Literature and Music* (Edinburgh, 2019). King Fisher: see J. Weston, *From Ritual to Romance* (Mythos Series ed.: Princeton, NJ, 1993), 113–36.

say in October 1945, were voices in the 'chorus of traditions' he wanted to 'incorporate and refashion' in the Masque. And if all that made for something of a blur at times, so be it. 'One can't manufacture a speculum for the deep things', he told Allinson, 'except out of indefiniteness.'[56]

56 Chorus of traditions: BL291.146 (21 Oct 1943): Sch 159. Speculum: *C20 Blues*, 168.

3 Collaboration on the Masque, 1943–44

How did Den Newton's concerns mesh with Tippett's when the collaboration-proper on 'our masque' began? Certainly the presence of things past—the underpinning and informing of modern life by myth and the artworks of other ages—appealed to him as it did to the composer. Witness not only that early experience of his with the *Lays of Ancient Rome* which had engendered a 'veritable fascination with the past', but also the poems he was writing in the 1940s, where past consciousness, notably as reflected in ancient Greek myth, poetry and sculpture or in the music and verse of the European Renaissance, is at once distant and close. ('Still the lovers lie between the sheaves/Though an enormous head glares through the soil.')[57] Again, the mighty opposites of the Masque's world—*anima* and *animus*, heaven and hell, dancing neophytes and a mechanic with a tool-kit—would surely have appealed, several of Newton's poems being formed of *yin-yang* presentations: day and night, summer and winter, land and sea, love and war, Utopia and Arcadia.[58] With the excitement of collaborating with an intimate friend on a large work made from such things outweighing any doubts he may have had about that friend's Jungian world-view, one can imagine him going with a will at helping Tippett to turn his basic story-line into a series of increasingly detailed scenarios and 'scripts' as a preliminary to his writing the Masque's libretto-proper for the composer to set.

Tippett hoped that they might 'risk a first sketch of the scenario' fairly soon after their collaboration began, with a view to working

57 Newton, 'Invasion Weather'; cf. his 'Archaic Art', 'A Death Mask', 'Songes and Sonnettes', 'Onionskin Man' and 'Disguises of the Artist' (see Appendix II for publication details).

58 E.g. 'Lacking a Guide', 'Landscapes of Night and Day', 'Cherubs of Venus', 'In St Anthony's Harbour' and 'Love and Wars of Mars and Venus' (see Appendix II).

further on it in Cambridge in early November 1943 and spending as much time as possible together in the months following. 'I can't quite see', he wrote that October, 'how we shall ever get at much real correspondence and collaboration without a period of very close union in a particular atmosphere.' In the event, they had to make do with snatched times in Cambridge, Surrey and London, with occasional holiday-time elsewhere and with the writing of many letters. In his, Tippett emerges understandably as the prime proposer of situations, psychologies and ideas for 'our masque', while Newton—in the roles of sounding board, source of stimulation, suggester of relevant texts, drafter of scripts and of course librettist-to-be—makes a contribution that the composer would later say had given him 'a great deal [...] in ideas and discussion': something he was bound to 'acknowledge [...] handsomely'.[59]

First on their agenda was the hunt for the dramatic 'gesture that corresponds' to each significant moment of the plot. Then, where the eightsome of *dramatis personae* was concerned, consideration had to be given to personal connections as one moved around the character-octagon or looked across its diagonals. This exercised Tippett especially in the case of the dancer Strephon, whom he saw as the man of instinctive intuition and creative imagination. In that connection he thought that the role should embody a 'concrete image' of the bisexuality that was appropriate to the artist. 'I have an idea', he wrote to Newton a few weeks into the collaboration, 'that the spiritual or artistic creativeness is of its own nature bisexual and it's useless to cry out against an apparently too concrete image of that fact.' The homosexual strand in that bisexuality had to be present, though without its being dominant. 'It's curious,' he goes on,

> that neither in the oratorio [*A Child of Our Time*] nor to any noticeable degree in the masque is queerness projected. In the masque it appears momentarily between two otherwise spliced males [= George and Strephon] (and I suppose we shall have to show its counterpart), but it's just about as much [queerness] as you have in yourself — i.e. no sexuality but candour and affection. And in the masque it stands as a gesture for a specific movement in the general dance — quite why I don't know. George kisses Strephon (the modern embraces the Greek!) to show his disregard of the

59 'First sketch': BL291.152 (29 Oct 1943). 'Close union': BL291.146 (21 Oct 1943): Sch 159. Appreciation and acknowledgement: see below, n. 134.

> conventional social barriers — from which the upheaval begins. And from that gesture he turns to Margaret, who spurns his sensuality for 'heaven'. A pretty good 'gesture' for the modern boy-girl relationship![60]

It's significant that Tippett feels the need to maintain symmetry in the octagon by showing a 'counterpart' to Strephon and George's closeness: an intimate sisterhood between Strephon's Girl and Margaret perhaps. But just what form that counterpart would take would depend on the collaborators' discovering the name of the Girl. 'If we succeed in naming her, she will as suddenly have a role'; the nature of Strephon's feelings for her will become clear too.[61] These are matters alluded to occasionally in sketchbooks and in the Tippett-Newton correspondence around this time, but they are left hanging rather.

Eager to communicate 'the Greek feeling', 'the Greek element' and its 'spring-like quality' as symbolised by Strephon, Tippett encouraged Newton to dip into Goethe and the 'Greece drunk' Hölderlin,[62] presumably having in mind the Hölderlin of big poems such as 'The Archipelago' and 'Bread and Wine', and the prose-paean to Ancient Athens in the novel *Hyperion*: vivid evocations of perfect Hellenic landscape and cityscape, climate, lifestyle, world-view and art. But Newton was keen too that Tippett should widen *his* reading, in his case in recent American literature. (Young Den after all was 'making his niche with American stuff'.) This was something that would have its effect on the plotting of the Masque.

It was Nick Moore, Newton's landlord at 86 Chesterton Road while Moore's parents were in the U.S.A. itself, who seems to have led the way in championing new and challenging U.S. writers. Prime among the figures he promoted were Henry Miller and Paul Goodman. Newton duly caught the Miller-Goodman bug (retaining it indeed till after the War, when he would publish short essays on both in the *New English Weekly*).[63] The anthologies co-edited by Moore and Newton,

60 BL291.147–8 (21 Oct 1943): Sch 159. Strephon's being descended in part from the half-mortal, half-fairy Strephon in Gilbert's *Iolanthe*—of which Newton had occasion to remind MT (BL292.7 [17 May 1944]: Sch 170)—will have familiarised him with half-and-half conditions.

61 BL292.8 (17 May 1944): Sch 170.

62 BL291.146 (21 Oct 1943): Sch 158.

63 *New English Weekly*, 30/10 (19 Dec 1946), 98–9, and 31/3 (1 May 1947), 27. In the latter, Newton writes that Goodman, 'the Jew, born in New York in 1911, boasts

the *Fortune* in 1942, the *Atlantic* in 1945, both include substantial pieces by and admiring salutes to Miller, and Goodman is welcomed warmly in the latter. In the years between, Newton was making sure that Tippett sampled both men's work, lending copies and, as Tippett's letters indicate, discussing them with him energetically. 'Greek' feelings were perhaps part of Newton's bait. Tippett certainly smiled on Miller's very Greek *Colossus of Maroussi*, quickly relating it to the Greek-German aspect of his and Newton's work-in-progress. ('The Greek elements in the masque need to be transmuted, not a romanticism; Hölderlin is like a very beautiful, classic Miller in the Greek stuff.')[64] About Goodman—libertarian, bisexual, 'anarcho-pacifist'—Tippett's feelings were more mixed.

Newton showed him several things: *Stop Light*, Goodman's sequence of modern American Noh-plays published in 1941; the big-city-based novel *The Grand Piano: or, The Almanac of Alienation*, of 1942; the short story 'Azazel' (in typescript-form presumably, since it wasn't printed until 1945 by Moore and Newton themselves in the *Atlantic Anthology*);[65] and the radical-in-subject-and-form fantasy-novel *Don Juan, or the Continuum of the Libido*, again in typescript. (It didn't see print until 1979; Goodman had presumably sent it across the Atlantic in the 1940s 'on spec', in the hope that some British publisher might be bold enough to take it on. None was.) The blend of ancient Japanese form and up-to-date Yankee content in Goodman's Noh pieces was something both Newton and Tippett were likely to respond to; indeed, the composer in autumn 1943 told Newton of his eagerness 'to talk of the Paul Goodman No play idea' along with *Maroussi*, their own Masque, Newton's new poems 'and masses of everything else — the sort of contact I like with you'. Newton doubtless thought that *The Grand Piano* would interest the pacifist composer since Lothair Alger, a principal character in it, is both composer and pacifist. Tippett might well have found its Chapter IV, on Lothair's politics and his problems with the civic and military authorities, particularly engaging, and it

himself a "novelist and regional poet" of that city. The minutiae of metropolitan life inform his work, to be refreshed by his choice and wonder, in their turn giving back to his scene a mythological glamour. A disciple of Marx and an anarchist, a student of Freud and deeply concerned with religion, Goodman works from the intellect: here is his individuality and his voice.'

64 BL292.10 (22 May 1944). MT recommended Miller's *Colossus* to John Layard, to Francesca Allinson also: *C20 Blues*, 142.

65 *Atlantic Anthology* (London, 1945), 103–17. A variant text of the story was published the same year in America in Goodman's *The Facts of Life*.

was probably the novel's presentation of Lothair's capitalist anti-self, the 'merchant prince' Hugo Eliphaz, that led to Tippett's describing a proposed aria or trio on bosses and workers in the Masque as 'a Goodmanesque affair'.[66] As for the short story 'Azazel' (which reworks the Biblical tale of the 'scapegoat' in a modern American setting), that would surely have had something to say to the presenter of another modern scapegoat in *Child of Our Time*, though the sins that Jimmy, Goodman's Azazel, encourages his young buddies to commit aren't race-connected so much as polymorphously perverse. As one of the buddies says, 'When we did not even know we desired the pleasures of bestiality or pederasty, what an effortless self-discovery it was for each one to see those taken for granted by our dear friend Jimmy!' The bestiality-pederasty pairing struck a dark chord with Tippett. When stressing to Newton the necessity of Natural Man's curbing the temptation to regress all the way to pure animal impulse, he was reminded of Newton's and Nick Moore's Americans. It is an issue 'now ripe to be understood', he says,

> that behind the stomach that moves is a complete Natural History — we accept that intellectually, but to accept it in fact of behavior means shock after shock — if not several prison sentences for paederasty and bestiality! Vide Henry Miller and the lesser dope Paul Goodman.[67]

Pederasty and bestiality recur in connection with regression in Tippett's reading of Goodman's *Don Juan*. Though he didn't think the book an artistic success, he did 'read a lot of it with amusement and a deal of it with an erection,' writing Newton two weighty letters about it. He found himself 'moved by the end more than any other portion': an end which must have reminded him of the Masque-in-progress,

66 'To talk of the Paul Goodman...': BL291.144 (18 Oct 1943). 'Goodmanesque': BL292.23 (20 June 1944). *Re* the idea of a 'Goodmanesque' number in the Masque, MT recalls in the same letter that 'Eisler and Brecht once did this, I believe, over Exchange Rate Value or something similar.' (Is he perhaps thinking of the 'Song of the Stimulating Impact of Cash' from their *Round Heads and Pointed Heads*?) MT's own proposed aria or trio may have mutated later into the duet for Jack and King Fisher in *Midsummer Marriage*: 'A job's a job, and there's no question'. For MT, Eisler and Brecht, see pp. 87–93 of S. Robinson, 'From Agitprop to Parable', in Robinson, ed., *Michael Tippett: Music and Literature*.

67 'When we did not even know...': 'Azazel' in Moore and Newton, eds., *Atlantic Anthology*, 103–4. 'Behind the stomach': BL291.197–8 (15 Feb 1944).

since it startlingly takes the form of the scenario-cum-libretto for what is virtually a Renaissance masque: a multi-media mythological ballet about Theseus and Ariadne that is by turns solemn, spectacular and comic, and that climaxes in a big debate between love and marriage, Eros and Hymen.[68] Tippett approved. In a letter of January 1944 he judged that

> the psychological technical regression in Don Juan to the classical mythology is correct — the regression to the period in which we were closer to the instincts, without our never to be disvalued, but dangerous intellect (a servant, but not a master, properly) — and where paederasty and bestiality were on much the same level as heterosexuality — a matter which *profoundly* offends our modern moral consciousness.

A sound moral consciousness was one which formed contentious but trusty henchmen of *both* idealistic intellect (with its sublime longings) and primal instinct (with its ungainsayable needs), for

> to attempt to live at the level of one's [idealistic] longing is to deny the earth-bound quality of all life — to lose all connection with the instincts and to stymie. And yet the longing (for heavenly perfection) remains too. A mystery.

Goodman's work is here being drawn into the linked spheres of Tippett's creativity and his intimate personal life. In the same January letter he connects the concern with regression with a dream he had recently had, in which

> I put my hand on a penis that was fleshy and that bounded about under the hand like something alive in its own right. [...] It was as though the tip were a fish's mouth and would nip my finger with its teeth.

The experience, he said, was 'like dreaming Goodman'. What the dream signified, he thought, was that

> if the practical intellectual finger comes in contact with the semen-producing organ of sex, then the way is not open thereby

68 'Read a lot of it': BL291.178 (9 Jan 1944). Mythological ballet: Goodman, *Don Juan*, ed. T. Stoehr (Santa Barbara, 1979), 145–60.

> to the world of the pure transcendental ideas, but to the world of natural history and the archaic animal past.[69]

Penis = toothed fish = past aeons of animal/human evolution. By great good fortune, Tippett discovered only a week later that the equation, seemingly so personal to him, was in part substantiated from several corners of the ancient world in a collection of highly erudite essays published in 1921, *Orpheus the Fisher: Comparative Studies in Orphic and Early Christian Cult Symbolism*, by Robert Eisler: a scholar to whose researches he could have been alerted by way of footnotes in admired books of Jung's and/or in the 'Fisher King' chapter of Weston's *From Ritual to Romance*. In three letters to Newton on three consecutive days at the beginning of February 1944, Tippett bubbles with excitement and creative stimulation about the discovery of a book in which there were phallic fish in Hindu, Babylonian, Latin, folk-German and other traditions. Best of all was the sacred *galeos* or shark of the Greeks, said 'to procreate in an irregular way, namely through the mouth' — a mouth of course with formidable teeth. Alongside the fish, Eisler gave stimulating attention to the symbolism of fishermen's barrels and nets. Five holy or magical finds in barrels are instanced (three Christian, two pagan), as are sundry mythical Greek, Jewish and Arabic nets in which a dozen fabulous objects were discovered at one time or another: 'the brass bottle with the jinn of the Arabian Nights in it', a 'cup of the Seven Sages' and so on. Even more exciting was Eisler's retrieval of a Babylonian *logos*-mystical text: 'Thy Word, the great net encircling heaven and earth.'[70] (His illustrations added to the fun: among them three Greek shark-priests; an ancient red-figured cup showing not only a submerged fisherman's barrel but also, to Tippett's delight, an ithyphallic satyr performing a remarkable balancing act, and—especially for Den—a Buddhistic *yoni* with 'two fishes and a figleaf [...] outlining it'.)

69 BL291.184 (23 Jan 1944): Sch *164–5. *Re* intellect and instinct, cf. one of Jung's clearest definitions of individuation, in *The Integration of the Personality*, tr. S. Dell (London, 1940), 27: 'Let it be a fair fight [between consciousness and the unconscious] with equal right on both sides. Both are aspects of life. Let consciousness defend its reason and its self-protective ways and let the chaotic life of the unconscious be given a fair chance to have its own way, as much of it as we can stand.'

70 Three letters on consecutive days: BL291.189–93 (1–3 Feb 1944): in part in Sch *165–7. (Sch omits a large part of the 2 Feb letter). Cf. Eisler, *Orpheus the Fisher* (London, 1921): fish, 256–64; *galeos*, 50; barrels and nets, 102–3; 'Thy Word', 73n.

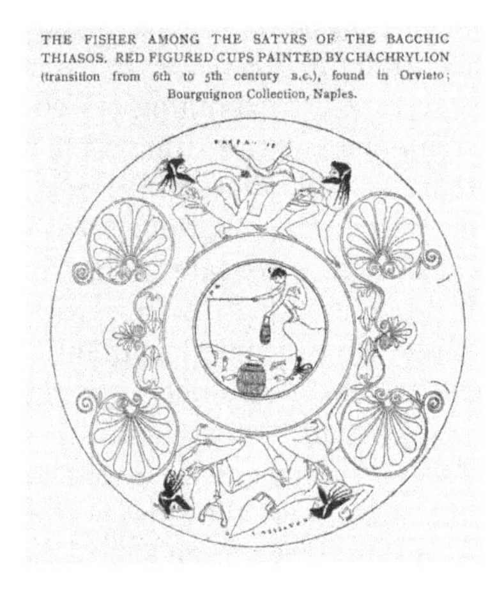

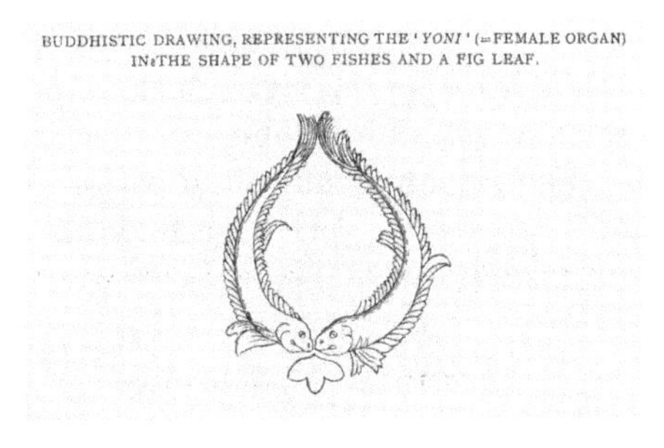

Image 3.1 Plates 17, 35 and 60 of Robert Eisler, *Orpheus the Fisher* (1921).

For a few days the nets and barrels distracted Tippett's attention from the sharp-toothed fish, perhaps because the nets stirred memories of a dream he had had five years before in February 1939 and had written up in the 'dream sequence' journal he kept that year. This featured a phantom choral work called *Magisches Netz und*

Fischeres,[71] and behind it lay his long-term, puzzled fascination with a cryptic poem of Goethe's, 'Die Magische Netz':

> Are they battles that I see?
> Are they games? Are they wonders?
> Five most splendid boys
> Against five kinsmen fighting.
> Regular, measured
> As a sorceress commands.
> They wield white spears
> Which weave quick threads [...]
> So with struggles, fights, victories
> Escape alternating with return
> An artful net is woven. [...][72]

In February 1944, as the Masque's scenario was being refined, Goethe's *Netz* may have blended in Tippett's imagination with the nets in Eisler, especially the Babylonian 'great net encircling heaven and earth'—(until he'd read *Orpheus the Fisher*, he said, he'd 'had no idea that the "net" is such a terrific symbol')—to become one of the wonders which would be revealed when King Fisher consulted the Ocean about his daughter's future. The Masque's net, he decided, was to be hidden in a magic barrel which was like the barrels in Eisler but had the additional gift—one it shared with sundry magic cauldrons in Celtic myth—of serving the folk who dip into it with their just deserts on a physical plane or with poetic/prophetic powers on a spiritual one. (Jung, for instance, cites the Irish Dagda's magic cauldron 'which supplies everybody with food according to his needs or merits', while Charlotte Guest's nineteenth-century *Mabinogion*-compilation features a Welsh cauldron whose contents allow Gwion, pre-incarnation of the great bard Taliesin, to foresee 'everything that was to come.')[73] Tippett wrote to Newton on February 2nd about these new plot-inspirations:

> I think the future (in the masque) is contained maybe in a large barrel, out of which Jack the practical man of his hands and fingers can find nothing. Strephon and his girl, the intuitive pair

71 *C20 Blues*, 84.

72 Text and translation in *C20 Blues*, 81–3. Cf. n. 175 below.

73 Jung, *Psychological Types*, 236n. Guest, *The Mabinogion* (Everyman's Library ed.: London, 1906), 263. For cauldron *loci* in myth, see pp. 114–6 of P. Henry, 'The Caldron of Poesy', *Studia Celtica* 14/15 (1979–80), 114–28.

> do a lovely dance around the barrel and eventually extract out of it a huge fishing net. It is this that exasperates King Fisher so that he orders Jack (as policeman [*scored through and replaced by* 'magician']) to remove Sosostris — which J. is unable to do and therefore K. strips off the veils himself and finds the pair coupled like an Indian God-Goddess. Jack by this time is changing his allegiance from the old to the new, so that he is no longer of use to K. I think that therefore K. obtains the revolver either out of Jack's police pocket or his own (the former, if Jack throws his uniform aside as an act of renunciation) [...] The shot magically kills K. and leaves the divine pair unassimilable — there follows the Dance of the Net in which they gradually tie up the pair (vide note to Don Juan!)[74] and carry them off, but of course they return from the other side of the stage at the same moment as George and Margaret. See Goethe's poem Magisches Netz for description of the net dance. The barrel in the finale contains wine of course.

So the net and the barrel get into the Masque. And the regressive fish with its Goodmanesque connections? Within a few hours of writing to Newton, Tippett changed his mind about Jack searching the barrel and finding nothing. Rather, he wrote the next day, 'Jack of course finds the barrel full of water — and [...] when he dips his hand in it to obtain the oracular object he is bitten by the hidden fish — and so refuses to proceed.' The toothed phallic sea-creature—validated by Tippett's 'dreaming Goodman', supported by Eisler's precedents, symbolic of the long ages of animal and human evolution—gives Jack such a shock that he runs for cover to nice cosy Bella so as to shut out the implicit Darwinian nightmare.

In Tippett's view, Eisler's book 'settle[d] it', firming up and supporting his choice of symbols for the part of the Masque that presents the Ocean's wonders to King Fisher and deepening his conviction, expressed in a letter to William Glock a year later, that the work as a whole would 'be in every way a conjunction and deposit of all sorts of ideas and interests and traditions — and somehow contemporary or artistic/symbolic even, into the bargain'.[75] Things were going so well that, only a few weeks after those productive excursions into recent American literature and ancient Eurasian religions, Tippett could

74 Goodman talks of 'netting' his material in an introductory note to *Don Juan*: known to Tippett from a (hypothetical) typescript but now to be found on p. 22 of Stoehr's 1979 published edition.

75 Schuttenhelm, *Selected Letters*, 255.

report to Newton that he had given Rose Mori, their typist, 'the first act of the Scenario and Commentary finished, to type,' and that he hoped 'to give her Act II by Thursday already — so that we may have the whole thing to chew on at the week end. In fact things move.'[76]

76 BL291.197 (15 Feb 1944).

4 The Act II scenario, *circa* February 1944

The hunt is still on for Rose Mori's typescripts, but we are lucky that a complete or near-complete scenario for Act II as envisaged at that time survives in manuscript in the second of Tippett's sketchbooks in the British Library. It's in a form clearly intended for a typist (NB the 'No new paragraph' at one point), and it's sometimes so close in its phrasing to parts of the composer's January and February letters to Newton as to warrant belief that it is the actual text Tippett hoped to give Ms Mori 'by Thursday'. Further, its highly discursive style suggests that when he writes to Newton of 'Scenario and Commentary', he means not two distinct documents but rather a plot-summary interspersed with profuse incidental comments — which is just what we have in this part of Sketchbook Two. A transcript follows, supported with some explanatory notes and cross-references.

As upbeat to it, the plot so far. In Act I we have been introduced to the choric Ancients and their singing and dancing Neophytes (Strephon among them), and in the Masque that the Ancients present to them we have seen George and Margaret meet, quarrel and go their separate ways, followed by the attempt of King Fisher and his entourage to run them down. The lovers have then returned, confronted each other and gone off on other journeys, which has mightily provoked King Fisher and set the boy- and girl-Neophytes against each other in argument. Then Act II:[77]

"[Sc 1.] The Windrose.[78]

The Wood. (Shadowy people passing half-seen in the distance.) The fact that [neither] the singing nor spectator chorus is there

77 Second Sketchbook, British Library Add. MS 72055, 2r-2v, 3v-6r, 7r-12r.

78 The placing and handwriting of this title ('windrose' = a compass-like diagram indicating wind directions and types) suggest that it may only have been written into

indicates that the episode is, as it were, outside time and space — the dream-land in which alone S[trephon] and his girl meet. It is also a portion of the archaic past of mankind to which the earth [*illegible*] by way of dances and fantasies. The portion that is not present is the Dionysiac frenzy, which nevertheless lies somewhere behind the Apollonian calm of the dance, so that the whole scene has a character of a ritual — one which has its very real dangers but where Strephon treads easily because of his natural instinctiveness.[79]

Sc 2. Entrance of Choruses, Kingfisher, Jack and Bella.

The singing chorus take their position as in Act I, followed by the dancing chorus. When they are all on, Kingfisher enters in his usual pompous manner attended by Jack and Bella.

Sc 3. Introduction of Mme Sosostris.

Kingfisher explains that, having failed to open the cave gates by mechanical means, he has decided to have recourse to another means. He intends to consult a clairvoyante: Mme Sosostris 'known to be the wisest woman in Europe'.[80] Consequently Jack has to be dressed by Bella as the priest-magician and between them they succeed in wheeling on a huge structure of black veils within which is Mme Sosostris, many times life-size. The monstrous veiled figure is placed in the stage centre.

Kingfisher, like the decaying society he personifies, can imagine no middle course between the 'things-are-what-they-are'[81]

---

the sketchbook later and may connect with the 'new choral and orchestral creation with a probable title of "The Windrose"', which MT said was 'germinating' in the spring of 1950 (White, *Tippett*, 63; cf. Bowen, *Michael Tippett*, 37) but which in the end he was not to write. (Newton however did write a windrose poem in 1944: 'Rose and Compass'; see Appendix I).

79 At the end of this scene, or so the last sentence of Sc. 9 of the Act II scenario implies, Strephon and his girl are—painfully for him—separated. MT jots on the back of an envelope for Newton two years later: 'Blackout after Strephon's dance. Chorus singing off.' BL292.162 (15 Feb 1946).

80 T. S. Eliot, *The Waste Land* (1922), I. 45; cf. *C20 Blues*, 90.

81 Cf. Wallace Stevens's long poem, 'The Man with the Blue Guitar', in the book (1937) of the same name: 'They said, "You have a blue guitar,/ You do not play things as they are"' (I. 3–4). In the 1940s Newton and Moore were pioneers in promoting Stevens's work in Britain, selecting poems of his (albeit not 'The Man with

attitude, and the crudest sentimental superstition. This is because the dissociation of sensibility is so acute: the intellect knows nothing of instinct, and vice versa.[82] Sosostris is the 'other world', or the chaotic unconscious of psychology, which Kingfisher imagines he can 'use' for his purposes, as he uses the practical intellect; personified here as Jack. Because he is quite sure the unconscious is 'nothing but - - - ' and that he fully comprehends it. He is not aware that the buried part of himself is also part of Sosostris and has led him unaware to the consultation to his inevitable undoing.

(George and Margaret have something of the same trouble when they are half-way through the drama at the Agon,[83] for here they try to use their experience of the super- and sub-natural to boost their egos against each other. The real heavenly light cannot be used to see with like a pocket-torch, but only to see our own iniquities with.)

Sc 4. The Consultation.

As soon as Sosostris is in place Kingfisher presents the problem to her, that he has lost his daughter, first apparently in heaven, now in hell. How is he to proceed, in order to find her.

Sosostris replies that if things have got to this stage of irrationality, one must proceed to the 'mythological drama' and bring the new attitude to birth: or words to that effect. K. is not of himself able to read the oracle. Appeal is made, therefore, to the 'ancients', who are presumed to know more about mythological affairs.[84] The 'ancients' interpret the oracle to mean that none of

---

the Blue Guitar') for their *Fortune* and *Atlantic* anthologies. MT would 40 years later write his own *Blue Guitar*—for guitar—after Stevens.

82 For 'dissociation of sensibility', see T. S. Eliot's 1921 essay, 'The Metaphysical Poets': 'The poets of the seventeenth century [...] possessed a mechanism of sensibility which could devour any kind of experience. [...] [But later in the century] a dissociation of sensibility set in, from which we have never recovered.' (Eliot, *Selected Essays*, 3rd ed. (London, 1951), 287–8. Cf. Eliot, *Varieties of Metaphysical Poetry*, ed. R. Schuchard (London, 1993), 29, 162 and 220–21.

83 It's likely that Tippett first came to be interested in 'Agons' ('struggles') through the 'Fragment of an Agon' in Eliot's *Sweeney Agonistes*; but this would have led him on, probably by way of Eliot's personal recommendation, to Sections V and VI—'*Agon*, Sacrifice, and Feast' and 'The Chorus in *Agon* and *Parabasis*'—of Francis Macdonald Cornford's *The Origin of Attic Comedy* (London, 1914 [hereafter '*Origin*']), 70–131.

84 For recourse to 'mythological drama', cf. n. 68 and associated main-text above. The drawing of the Ancients, the Masque's presenters, into the Masque itself may derive in part from avant-garde theatre-pieces earlier in the century where

the conventional methods of approach will enable Margaret to be released from hell, but only a radically new approach. And what the new thing is can only be discovered from the age-old keeper of secrets, the hidden depths of the sea.[85]

Jack therefore, dressed by Bella as fisherman-diver, is sent to the bottom of the sea to fetch a sample of it, which he presently rolls onto the stage inside a huge barrel. In psychological terms, the loss of [K.'s] daughter in hell means the loss of his soul, i.e. the relationship to the instincts and the unconscious in general. Consequently the serviceable intellect (Jack) must be taken from the practical everyday tasks for the moment, and be sent to the bottom of the sea. This is the traditional or mythological art which Kingfisher has forgotten and which is yet his proper paternity as shown by his name.[86] (For the whole immense psychology of the fish – fisherman – nets – Dionysus – wine – milk – music and whatnot else, vide Eisler, Orpheus the Fisher, London 1921.) Jack already approaches the divine art of the 'fisher' when dressed as magician-priest. A bishop's mitre is a fish-head, and identical with pictures of priests dressed as 'fishes' in a fertilisation rite depicted on ancient Babylonian seal-cylinders (loc. cit. above, plates X, XVI). As a magician Jack also displays his dramatic kinship to Mephistophilis in the Faust legend, and further back to Hermes-Psychopompos. One needs all one's sharpest faculties in order to 'dare the grave passage'![87]

Sc 5. The Fishing.

When the barrel has been placed on end in front of and below Sosostris, she orders it to be opened. This Jack is able to do,

---

narrator-figures are eventually drawn into the action, e.g. the Ramuz-Stravinsky *Histoire du Soldat* and André Obey's *Viol de Lucrèce*.

85 Cf. pp. 65–72 of Jung, *Integration of the Personality* (a book that MT—*C20 Blues*, 89—found 'absorbing'). MT quotes at length from these pages (in Jung's original German) in his 'Sketch for a Modern Oratorio', in relation to the chorus that begins Part 3 of *A Child of Our Time*. See Bowen, *Tippett on Music*, 168.

86 For the benign power of the true Fisher King, to which by implication the Masque's King Fisher should aspire, see Weston, *From Ritual to Romance*, 125–8 and 135–6. In a later letter to Newton (BL 292.94: March 1945), MT explains that 'the play is on [King Fisher's] name, and so the visit to the deep sea is as it were postulated in the story-names ab initio'.

87 'The grave passage': from MT's libretto for *A Child of Our Time*, Part 3 (the General Ensemble: 'I would know my shadow and my light').

though he has first to break Solomon's seal, which is upon it.[88] Sosostris then demands that someone put their hand into the interior and feel what they can find. Jack rolls up his sleeve and does so, but withdraws his hand with a shout, presumably having been bitten by a hidden fish within. He goes away to 'cry on Bella's shoulder' and flatly refuses to try again. Sosostris gives no indication as to what is to be done in this difficulty, but the 'ancients' opine that Jack is far too removed from the mythological nature of the process, and that K. Must have recourse to someone less sophisticated. Consequently, Strephon is called upon to 'fish'. This he does at the culmination of a ritualistic-looking dance, and out of a now apparently dry barrel produces a large fishing net which he unfolds with the help of the dancing chorus.

Jack as the intellect can break open the barrier between the conscious everyday world and the world of fantasy. But when the practical finger touches the fish (the 'phallos', the generative principle), it receives a shock. Because the truth is that the phallic instincts do *not* lead to the world of the Transcendental Ideas, but the world of Natural History. And while we can intellectually believe we are descended from animals (Darwin), we only truly experience this by actually entering the animal past — with moral consequences which are a perpetual affront to our protestant puritanism. Therefore the modern man, conceiving of himself as so civilised, withdraws, as Jack withdraws, into a sentimentality, pictured as the motherly woman housekeeper and bedmate. This is the fundamental protestant split.[89] (Of course the Dionysiac frenzy is not really accounted for by being left in the barrel. It breaks out as a[n] orgy of blood in total war.)

It should also be noted that, if the fish is the phallus, then to handle it is both a symbol of the most inferior sexual operation and of self-fertilisation, and hence of re-birth.[90] (No new paragraph.)

88 Solomon's seal: the leaden seal fixed by Solomon on a copper bottle to imprison a Djinn in the *Arabian Nights* tale, 'The Fisherman and the Djinn', instanced in the list of myths and tales in Eisler (*Orpheus the Fisher*, 102–3): a list MT transcribes for Newton (Sch 166).

89 In his commentary on Wilhelm's translation of *The Secret of the Golden Flower*, 127, Jung sees getting the rights of the unconscious into proper balance with the rights of consciousness as something that 'stands in violent opposition to the Western Christian, and especially to the Protestant, cult of consciousness.'

90 From 'But when the practical finger…' to '… hence of re-birth', several phrases echo those in MT's letters to Newton of 23 Jan and 2 Feb 1944 (*vid. sup.*).

'Und der Haifisch, der hat Zähne', as the opera has it: and sharks were the sacred fishes of the ancient Orphic initiations, which propagated through the mouth. (Ovid)[91] Strephon's 'fishing' represents a shift in the attitude represented by Jack getting his finger bitten. (Intellect contrasts with instinct: conscious becomes aware of un-conscious.) Consequently (as in dreams) there is no longer a shark or crab in the barrel, which is dry, and instead the net by which the drama can proceed.

Sc 6. The Unveiling of Sosostris.

Kingfisher is exasperated (as well he might be!) by the 'mythological drama', up to date, and begins to get in a temper. It there *appears* as though Sosostris trips him or gives him a push so that in the next instant K is struggling *in* the net, as held by Strephon and the chorus. When he has been disentangled he is in a towering rage and orders Jack to unmask the 'veiled woman'. Jack, who is getting fed up and 'revolutionary', reluctantly allows Bella to begin dressing him as the policeman. But when she comes to buckle on a holster and pistol-belt he really rebels, throws the belt and holster at K., who is down L., and after it the jacket, etc., and himself goes with Bella down R. K. now beside himself, rushes at Sosostris, and despite the darkening and rolls of drums begins to tear off the veils as seen by a spotlight. As the last veil comes off the wire frame, Sosostris is not disclosed, but George and Margaret, embracing in god-like garments of gold and other colours. Jack's bitten finger and Strephon's net represent a tremendous gain to the unconscious. Hence the conscious awakens to war. Kingfisher seeks to overpower the unconscious once for all by the Jack-ian intellect. But the intellect cannot contain the instinct or comprehend the mysterious. So the ego throws itself in a last desperate endeavour on the 'evil thing'. But just as K, by actually having to touch the veils is forced into contact, and to unveil the mystery, so in the new-born world George and Margaret, who have been as far apart as heaven and hell, re-appear united.

91 'Und der Haifisch...': 'The Ballad of Mack the Knife' – Prologue to Brecht-Weill, *The Threepenny Opera* (1928). Ovid: *recte* pseudo-Ovid, vv. 107–8 of the *Halieutica* once attributed to him; cf. Eisler, *Orpheus the Fisher*, 38–9 and 50.

(Presumably George and Margaret slip behind the veils and Sosostris gets off stage during the fuss disentangling K from the net.)

Sosostris is no longer there of course, because as Ghost, she disappears after the manifestation of power.

(K has never meditated on these profound words seen in a book review: Beware Miss Tennyson Jesse.[92] The world turns on its axis, and it is hard to know who is the right way up and who hangs upside down.)

Sc 7. The Apotheosis of the Protagonists.

On seeing his daughter in the arms of George Kingfisher rushes down left to where the police uniform and the holster lie. He takes out the revolver and despite a cry from Jack prepares to shoot George. (Spotlights outline a triangle, with G. and M. as the apex, and K. and J. as the points of the base.) But when he actually fires, George lifts his hand with the palm turned towards K. (in the manner of an Indian god) at the identical moment, and K. falls dead as the shot is heard.

After momentary consternation Jack and Strephon and the chorus lift up the body as on a bier and slowly carry it (to a dirge) upstage C, and lay it down there, behind G. and M., who above the ground-bass of the dirge sing an ecstatic coloratura duet. (All the stage lighting is still of the spot-light type.)

K. in this scene becomes like the various modern rulers, drunk with power, and finds his own nemesis, thus personifying the inevitable self-destruction of the so-called Christian Civilisation the Western world enjoys. In this connection it is perhaps no accident that G. and M. appear in the attitudes of an Eastern god and his mate.[93] The sounding together of the dirge for the old and the song of the new also gives a musical picture of the light backed by the shadow, in natural and proper relation to one another. K. is taken upstage towards the land of the 'idea'. G. and M. are of course non-human: in psychological terms completely inflated by the collective ideas of conscious and unconscious, which have entirely submerged the small area where a personal ego is able to sustain itself. The problem therefore is how to re-humanise them.

92 Fryniwyd Tennyson Jesse (1888–1958), novelist and playwright; something of a sibyl where matters criminological were concerned.

93 For a possible link with Jung on Shiva and Shakti, see n. 178 below.

Facilis descensus Averni;
Noctes atque dies patet atri junua Ditis.
Sed revocare gradem superasque evadere ad auras
Hoc opus, hic labor est.[94]

Sc 8. The Net Dance.

Either silently or vocally the 'ancients' direct operations towards the Net Dance. The net is taken up by the chorus and energetically by certain of them standing on the edge of the podium and holding the net out at arms' length above their heads while others hold the net at stage level. The net appears like a huge carpet on end, and indeed is not opaque — the veils having been taken up as a backing in front of which the pattern of the net shines in small squares and knots. When the carpet effect is ready, the whole contraption is let down over G. and M., and the net drawn to by the cords, and the net and its contents then thrown into the orchestra pit — or down the cave mouth — or elsewhere. As the bundle is thrown away (or burnt!) the lights go up and G. and M. are seen in their ordinary clothes coming hand in hand from upstage C. behind the corpse of Kingfisher. They shake hands all round — at least metaphorically.

The 'mythological drama' [proposed by Sosostris] is of course the drama of Act II itself. This scene is the point of un-ravelling, the appearance of the deus ex machina — only it appears as a netting. An extraordinary series of wonder objects (the treasures of the sea, i.e. the unconscious) is found in the nets of mythology. But the dance in the form of a net is the poem of Goethe: Magisches Netz[95] — when the boys and girls dancing release and retake individual members of the group in series — forming thereby the magical net of the poem. In this sense the net is the symbol of what knits or knots us together as a fraternity.

(Presumably G. and M. escape off stage while the net hangs in the air as a carpet.)

94 Virgil, *Aeneid* VI. 126–9: the Sybil telling Aeneas that it's easy enough to get into the underworld, far less easy to get out of it. MT would have encountered these lines quite recently as the epigraph to Ch. 4 ('Dream Symbols of the Process of Individuation') of Jung, *Integration of the Personality*, 96, where they evoke the effort needed to come fully through the individuation process.

95 Letting down the net: cf. Eisler, *Orpheus the Fisher*, 262. Wonder objects: see n. 70 above. 'Magisches Netz': see n. 72 and associated text.

Sc 9. The Mock Doctor.

G. and M. are very pleased with themselves being still somewhat contaminated with their god-like status. All the young people congratulate them, and the chorus. But the 'ancients' point out that while it has been very nice to have been to heaven and hell, and been reborn, etc. the trouble of such experiences is that they divorce us from our everyday responsibilities and human susceptibilities. Chorus-Mistress (to Margaret): 'You show not the slightest feeling from your heart, even awareness that your spiritual pride has in fact killed your father.'

Consequently Jack and Bella undergo their final transformation, into Doctor and Nurse, and play the old Mummers' drama of bringing the 'King of Egypt' back to life, who has been slain by St George (Margaret being, of course, 'the King of Egypt's daughter').[96] K only comes 'alive' in a remote fashion and is propped up at the C[entre] back with his paper crown and sceptre.

There might be a mock lamentation first.

G. and M. are still somewhat 'inflated', and need a jolt or two to bring them back to ordinary life. Nevertheless all the young ones receive an increase of life from K's death.[97] Also the distance of their world of something new struggling through chaotic convulsion to birth, and the old world of K., or even the 'ancients', is now reduced. So that divisions are for the moment overcome, 'even that false, artificial estrangement which has cursed our century, of youth from age'.[98] This is expressed by the bringing of K. to life and crowning him: and by the easier tone of the 'an-

96 Cornford points out a link between the 'resurrections' in Aristophanic comedy and those in the Mummers' drama: *Origin*, 87. In numerous English Mummers' plays, St George boasts that he 'fought the fiery dragon and drove it to the slaughter', so winning 'the King of Egypt's daughter'. Occasionally an actual Egyptian King makes an appearance (though when he does it's very rare that he is slain and revived). In a section of libretto-draft in the First Sketchbook (Add. MS 72054, 8r), the Mumming-play connection is knowingly kept up with a line of Margaret's to George: 'Father comes home from Egypt today.'

97 For Cornford's ideas about the rejuvenation of agonists and even choruses near the ends of Aristophanic comedies, see *Origin*, 87–93. For George and Margaret's return to ordinary life, cf. Layard, *The Lady of the Hare*, 52, on adjusting a patient to the quotidian after deep analysis: 'The analytical process is itself like the Mass and like all true ritual as well as great works of dramatic art, in that it leads to peaks of emotion from which the participant has to be led back from scenes of glory very gently into the realms of everyday life, lest the sudden contrast damage the soul.'

98 Quotation-source yet to be traced.

cients'. But whether Strephon gets his girl and the boy-girl division of the chorus ceases at this point, I do not know.[99]

Sc 10. The Sun Dance.

Strephon, looking rather like the resuscitated Adonis,[100] leads a general round dance.

The barrel now contains wine! George and Jack dispense it; not forgetting a libation to the stone faun.[101]

After integration the new 'sun' rises on the horizon. ('It is spring.') The new day will of course eventually reach noon, at which hour, the Chinese observe, night begins.[102]

In every scene the concerted music only begins when the words no longer matter, and where the drama lies in the situation and the gesture. Whether actual speech is used, as in 'Zauberflöte', and recitative as a first musical plane — or all recitative — is a matter for discussion.[103] The reason why the singing-chorus cannot be the same people as the dancing-chorus (which need not be large) is because the chorus *action* needs to [be] so stylised and dance-like."

99 Boy–girl choric division: see n. 114 and related main-text.

100 See Frazer, *The Golden Bough*: Chs. 6 ('Adonis') and 8 ('Ritual of Adonis') of Book II, *Killing the God.*

101 See n. 106 and related main-text.

102 'It is spring': further allusion to the General Ensemble, 'I would know my shadow...', in *Child of Our Time.* 'The Chinese observe ...': probably alluding to Jung's paraphrase of the *I Ching*: 'When *yang* has reached its greatest strength, the dark power of *yin* is born within its depths; night begins at midday when *yang* breaks up and begins to change to *yin.*' (Wilhelm, *Secret of the Golden Flower*, 85.)

103 The upshot of the discussion at that stage, as we shall see, was the decision to use speech, recitative, song and chorus — all four.

5 Friends' reactions and progress of the collaboration, 1944–46

The Act II scenario in the sketchbook gives us the plot as roughed out in some detail quite early in 1944: a plot which, as far as we know, stayed broadly the same till spring 1946. The months between allowed time for considerations of form and genre, and for small modifications, revisions, experiments and riffs as part of the movement towards a more sophisticated scenario, and to the writing of what Tippett called a 'script': a detailed, continuous narrative of actions, ideas and sketched utterances which could subsequently be refined into the precise words of the libretto Newton would write. Thus Tippett could tell Allinson, probably in mid-spring 1944, that

> Den was here yesterday — Sunday — and we went at the Masque and have made decisions as to where and what people sing. [...] It's important progress towards the clothing, and means that he can begin to try his hand at a scene or two. Much less speech than I had foreseen and more singing.[104]

In all of this, the February scenario (the half of it we have at least) made a good first draft, though there were lacunae in it. For instance, it revealed little about Strephon and less about his Girl, beyond showing that they have a pre-scene in which they dance ritualistically in a dimension of their own and then seemingly move apart. In the weeks that followed the typing, Tippett's letters suggest, he and Newton went on puzzling over the pair. One idea that came up was that Strephon and the Girl 'never really meet' — that's to say never humanly interact. (If so, it struck Tippett that the Girl's name could be Psyche, after the girl in Apuleius' *Golden Ass* whose encounters with Cupid are in pitch darkness.) Or she might be solely an idea of Strephon's. The composer's

104 MT, letter to Allinson (private collection).

close friend Evelyn Maude suggested that her 'indefiniteness [...] really means that he isn't paired at all, that he subsumes her into himself.' Tippett was reluctant to go quite that far, as he had 'always had a pas-de-deux in my vision': one that Strephon would dance with 'the complementary figure, whatever that is'. He agreed, though, that

> it may be right that she has no name and is always Strephon's girl — and I am pretty sure that they do not pair in the general marriage, but are eternally separate. [...] Not biologically paired, [they are] paired out of their selves — being both mixtures. Which makes Jack and Bella the fertile pair, and [Jack] the Natural Man.

The character-octagon is clearly still at the back of his mind here: its principal pair's diagonal intersected at one angle by a 'mixture'-pair and at another by a natural-fertile pair, with King Fisher and Sosostris (an Oedipal pair, he would come to think) at right-angles to them. Of course Maude's suggestion, if adopted, would upset the octagon. There would have to be a new Character No. 8 to complement Strephon. Still, by that stage a Faun had made his way into the plot, and Tippett allowed that things might possibly be arranged so that 'the faun is the 8th character'.[105]

There are only a few glancing allusions to this Faun in surviving letters, and just two in the sketchbooks. Put together, they imply that he—sometimes 'it'—is a stone statue holding a flute who comes alive on occasion and plays for the dancers; that he may be part of some kind of triangle with Strephon and his Girl (named in this connection Parthenia, seemingly on the advice of Nick Moore's philosopher father, now back in Cambridge); and that he turns to stone in very short order when mortals appear, but in that state is worthy of their homage as a work of art associated with the cult of Dionysus (so complementing Strephon, whose dance with the Girl in the Act II scenario is 'Apollonian'). Such a profile fits a draft fragment of script in Tippett's Third Sketchbook:

> B[ella] enters. Dance stops. P[arthenia] vanishes, disappears.
> F[aun] goes to stone.

105 'Never really meet' and 'Psyche': BL292.10 (22 May 1944). (Sch, who at pp. 154–5 prints much of the letter though not this part of it, dates it as 14 Sept 1943; but the BL's suggestion of 22 May 1944—misread by Sch as 22 September—fits better, following in sequence as it does on the 17 May 1944 letter.) 'Isn't paired at all', 'has no name' and '8th character': BL292.7 (17 May 1944): Sch 170. 'Natural man': cf. Wilhelm, *Golden Flower*, 71.

B: Jack Jack.
J: What is it? (S[trephon] runs off)
B: Did you see him?
J: Who? the dancer Strephon?
B: I could have sworn I saw a girl with him just now.
She must have vanished.
J: You're getting jumpy, Bella and seeing things.
B: Perhaps. I was not born for all these mysteries.

And a sketch of Tippett's for the Masque's finale in a letter to Newton includes the Faun 'taking the musical instrument forever to his stone lips' and receiving the libation also mentioned at the end of the 1944 scenario.[106] As for his ancestry, it's arguable that, much as the Ancients derive from Bernard Shaw and Mme Sosostris from T. S. Eliot, so the Faun comes from Nathaniel Hawthorne. Tippett read Hawthorne as a young man, and Newton would have found the American's 1860 novel *The Marble Faun*—the first third of it at least—very much to his taste, with its visits to sculpture galleries and evocations of ancient art. The book's central conceit is that the flute-carrying 'Faun' of Praxiteles is in some sense alive in one of its modern characters: a young count from deepest Tuscany, spontaneous, beautiful, half-human, half-animal and untroubled by that condition.[107]

Evelyn Maude had another suggestion when she was shown the February scenario: that the collaborators should change their provisional title for it, *The Masque of Revolution*. Tippett, who came to hold that 'the real revolution of our time [lay in] the discovery and invention of the unconscious', doubtless saw the Revolution in that title as primarily a matter of the triumph of Jungian individuation in the psychological domain, albeit with a social-political dimension (reflecting Tippett's earlier Trotskyist phase) in Jack's boss-rejecting change of heart and the overthrow of King Fisher. But Maude thought the title 'unnecessary' and 'confusing', and held that it would do the Masque no good. Bowing to this, the collaborators reverted to 'the 2 very nice other titles' they had earlier come up with: *Aurora Consurgens* and *The Laughing Children*.[108] Their Eliotesque Laughing Children

106 BL292.14 (7 June 1944); BL292.131 (19 Sept 1945); BL292.115 (? Summer 1946): Sch 183; Third Sketchbook: Add. MS 72056, 40r; Second Sketchbook: Add. MS 72055, 11v.
107 MT reads Hawthorne: *C20 Blues*, 248. Praxiteles' *Faun* alive: Hawthorne, *The Marble Faun*, intro. R. Brodhead (London, 1990), 7–14, 70–71 etc.
108 'The real revolution…': MT, *Moving into Aquarius*, 111. 'Nice other titles…': BL292.7 (17 May 1944): Sch 170.

were the chorus of observing, commenting, sometimes mocking young Neophytes who watch the Masque-proper; so the title chimed with those of several comedies by Aristophanes memorable for their choruses: *The Birds, The Wasps, The Clouds* and such. As for *Aurora Consurgens* ('the rising dawn'), that was the name of an anonymous medieval treatise on alchemy once ascribed to St Thomas Aquinas and resuscitated in the mid-1930s by Jung, who alludes to it in one of his 'Eranos' essays, 'The Idea of Redemption in Alchemy': an essay first published in German in the *Eranos Jahrbuch 1936* and then included in his 1940 English collection, *The Integration of the Personality*. (Tippett very likely first encountered it in the German, since he read the Year-books as they came out.) The Latin phrase derives from the image *consurgens ut aurora*, which is used, alongside images of the sun and moon, to describe the Beloved in the Biblical *Song of Solomon*. ('Who is this arising like the dawn?') The treatise itself applies the phrase to Sophia, the goddess-like Spirit of Wisdom, said to permeate profound alchemical thought; Jung makes his own use of it in 'The Idea of Redemption' when he suggests that, assisted by the study of alchemy's psychological aspects, we may

> come upon the fundamental psychic facts that remain unchanged for thousands of years. [...] From this point of view, modern times and the present appear as episodes in a drama that began in dark prehistory, and that runs through the centuries towards a distant future. The drama is an *aurora consurgens*: humanity's coming to consciousness.[109]

A masque of *Aurora Consurgens* by Tippett and Newton could not only present the dawning of that consciousness across its whole action; it could also feature physical-musical presentations of dawns actually arising as its opening and closing 'gestures'. 'Right at the very start', Tippett told Barbara Hepworth a decade later, 'I saw, in a kind of vision, the scenic apparatus of an apparently commonplace sunrise, transmuted unexpectedly into a symbol of all that is to come'; in 1945 he tried out one version of the closing scene on Newton: 'The final lighting of the cyclorama, after the libation [...] and the last great trill of the voices and orchestra, is some sort of dawnlike light, not an

109 *Song of Solomon* 6:10. *Eranos-Jahrbuch 1936* (Zürich, 1937), 103 (cf. 62 and 85–6), as tr. in Jung, *Integration of the Personality*, 269. MT reads the *Yearbooks*: Bowen, *Tippett on Music*, 228. See also A. Haaning, 'Jung's Quest for the *Aurora Consurgens*', *Journal of Analytical Psychology* 59/1 (2014), 8–40.

evening but a before-morning feeling.'[110] In stage technique and musical invention, these great dawns would be spectacles worthy of the Masque's big ideas of consciousness-making, and worthy of the traditions of the court masques under King Charles I, shows which themselves had occasionally used elaborate lighting effects—for instance there's an early-dawn scene in Shirley's *Triumph of Peace* (1634) that involves a spirit in a moving cloud—and had sported learned Latin titles too: *Coelum Britannicum, Luminalia, Salmacida Spolia.*

John Amis, David Ayerst and Francesca Allinson, good friends of the collaborators, were also shown the scenario in spring 1944, and their responses arguably influenced *Aurora*'s developments over the next two years. Though Tippett could report in March that 'reading the Masque Scenario last night [I] considered it a cert', he had to give Newton and Allinson the 'dampening' news around the same time that Amis considered it 'a private joke on 5th form psychology and [...] a waste of possibly good music'. Tippett thought that Amis had missed the theatrical point: he 'can't visualise it as a stage do, because he thinks that it would make a good story — which is precisely what it wouldn't do. It isn't a story at all, but a mime — an allegory in modern technique.'[111] In that allegory, King Fisher, for instance, is decaying society ('the so-called Christian civilisation the Western world enjoys'), Strephon instinctive imagination, and the 'natural man' Jack is serviceable intellect. (Tippett saw Jack at this stage as alienated in the Marxist sense: as 'nearly a caricature of the modern man who is only understood as his job, his social value, and has no rounded human value permitted by the nature of our society.') As for 'modern technique', Tippett makes bold to blend different ages, religions and ideologies, for instance, in the presentation of his principal lovers when they appear semi-transfigured after their first journeys in Act I. With Margaret,

> something is taken from St Joan, the virginal knight in white armour, and something from Pallas Athene — her confidence with coldness. But these older modes are oddly mixed with allusions to the New Woman and the Schoolmistress. [With George,] something has been taken from Faust, the impious magician-lover,

110 MT to Hepworth: Schuttenhelm, *Selected Letters*, 353–4; MT to Newton: BL292.131 (19 Sept 1945).

111 'A cert': BL291.211 (21 March 1944). Dampener from Amis: *C20 Blues*, 167 and BL291.205 (March 1944).

> something from Dionysus — his feminine, spring-like beauty that can be distorted with bestial frenzy. But these older modes are oddly mixed with allusions to the film-star and the Commando.[112]

Still, though secure with his masque-style personifications, Tippett may have been nudged by Amis's criticism into wondering whether he and Newton might bring forward the narrative element of the piece and round out its characters — might move it, that is to say, towards 'opera' without compromising its original conception. In mid-May 1944 he was allowing in a letter to William Glock that *Aurora* might be labelled an 'opera-masque'[113] (with a nod perhaps to the Cocteau-Stravinsky 'opera-oratorio' *Oedipus Rex*); later that year he and Newton were looking at Francis Cornford's *Origin of Attic Comedy* with a view to some solid opera-building.

Tippett had consulted the *Origin* (and been struck by its concept of the 'agon') close to his time in Wormwood Scrubs the year before, almost certainly on the recommendation of T. S. Eliot, who admired the book and had drawn on the conventions it discusses in his *Sweeney Agonistes*. But now the collaborators were wanting to look in detail at Cornford's analysis of the construction of an Aristophanic drama. In July, keen to consult a public-library copy, Tippett wrote to Newton from Devon (soon after the death of his father there): 'Could you manage somehow to remember the Cornford book and bring.' Then later:

> The Cornford shows how luckily the masque has fallen into traditional shape, and it gives me various fresh details and relevances which I can annotate into my [scenario-] copy, along with the notes of music intended, and then show you. [...] [The Greek dramatic] tetralogy [is] Agon: Death: Resurrection: Marriage. (Symphony?). Which [in *Aurora Consurgens*] might mean debate: defeat: return: ribaldry, with the 2 inside sections as the most fluid. So we could probably use this successfully in the [???] sequence.

Around the same time he suggests that they need to give form to the mayhem they had envisaged for the end of Act I by creating 'a choral Agon, the Parabasis of ritual' (*parabasis* being the direct address of the ancient chorus to the audience).

112 MT on Jack: Schuttenhelm, *Selected Letters*, 257–8. On Margaret and George: Second Sketchbook, Add. MS 72055, 22v.

113 Schuttenhelm, *Selected Letters*, 255.

> The chorus, united, which is judge and spectator of [George and Margaret's] individual Agon, after the disappearance of the Agonists breaks into two halves (boys — girls) and offs with the upper garments and has a set-to — till I suppose the ancients chase them off.

After which homage to the quarrelsome chorus of women *vs* men in Aristophanes' *Lysistrata*, the Ancients themselves would

> come slowly downstage and disrobe. They declare themselves as Poetry and Music, the joint creators, [and announce that] they have no truck with 'that - - - Suffolk Grimes or those - - - sickly children of our times'. There is a musical quotation from each [i.e. from *Peter Grimes* and *Child of Our Time*] — to which they listen attentively and sing: 'No, No, not that! pah!!'[114]

With the beginnings of a firm structure and with some fences and sign-posts from Cornford, 'the next step', Tippett thought, was 'to activate, concretise or even personify the sections'. And some months later: 'The job now is always the further humanisation of the framework.' Humanisation implied deepening the *dramatis personae*, and Tippett at this time was certainly showing greater interest in the characters *as* characters. Strephon, Sosostris and King Fisher, for example:

> Strephon reminds me a bit of Nijinsky – less sophisticated. If a woman forces copulation on him he is in the end sent off his head and destroyed — the balance of his creativeness being of another order. So we'd better leave Strephon with only a shadow partner. I don't want him to go off his head and write another diary.[115] We mustn't maltreat him so. [...] I've also 'seen' that Sosostris is in some way the mother-figure to Kingfisher, who is Oedipus: but I haven't guessed yet how this is objectified in word or gesture.

114 Eliot's admiration for Cornford: C. Ricks and J. McCue, eds., *The Poems of T. S. Eliot* (London, 2015), 1.785–6. (See pp. 225–7 of Kemp, *Tippett*, for a lucid exposition of the Cornfordian elements in the final *Midsummer Marriage* of 1952.) 'Remember the Cornford book': BL292.39 (July 1944). 'The Cornford shows...': BL292. 136 (mid-1944; the BL's proposed dating of this letter is 22 Aug 1945, but its wartime contents—the 'doodlebugs' especially—strongly suggest summer or autumn 1944). 'A choral Agon': BL292.38 (28 July 1944). Ancients disrobing: BL292.24 (20 June 1944). 'Parabasis': see Cornford, *Origin*, Sect. VI.

115 *The Diary of Vaslav Nijinsky*, edited by his wife Romola, had been published in 1936.

Margaret is probed in even more detail:

> Margaret is looking for the individuality suppressed by social collective values. She refuses G. because he represents marriage, refuses K[ing Fisher] because he represents duties to parents. It is only then that she is driven to concretise her behavior irrationally and transcendentally as the Search for the Land of the Sunrise. Her illusion is that she will be satisfied with a denial of the collective ties by the mystical loneliness of contemplation of the self.

By mid-1945 Tippett could report to Glock that 'the story is taking on more naturalistically human dressing and the allegorical and mythological element is receding behind. It constantly gets warmer.' And so gets more operatic? It seems yes. 'There's absolutely no doubt in my mind that it is an opera,' he had written to Newton some months earlier. 'As things are going along now, it all takes on more characterization and easy comedy and the allegorical, mythological element is less obtrusive.'[116]

David Ayerst would have been happy with such developments. His initial reaction to the scenario in spring 1944 seems to have been cool, and Tippett jokily reported to Allinson that 'there's a hell of a lot of rubbishy mythology in [*Aurora*] that gives David the creeps.' But Tippett told Newton in August that Ayerst had re-read the scenario 'and was converted to it', though (like the composer himself by this stage) 'he doesn't think it should be called a masque'.[117] It was probably around this time that the collaborators sketched the title-page for a projected printed libretto. It makes a clear announcement of the work's genre as well as its authorship:[118]

Douglas Newton
An Opera
in 2 Acts
AURORA CONSURGENS
or
The Laughing Children
MICHAEL TIPPETT

116 'To activate...': BL292.136. 'The job now...': BL292.122 (26 June 1945). Strephon-Nijinsky: BL292.7 (17 May 1944): Sch 170. Sosostris-King Fisher: BL292.90 (21 Feb 1945). Margaret: BL292.22 (20 June 1944). MT's report to Glock: Schuttenhelm, *Selected Letters*, 258. 'It is an opera': BL292.24 (20 June 1944).

117 Ayerst cool: BL291.217 (2 April 1944): Sch 168. Ayerst converted: BL292.50 (20 Aug 1944): Sch 176. 'Rubbishy mythology': *C20 Blues*, 168.

118 First Sketchbook: Add. MS 72054, 2v-3r.

— followed by what at this stage was a very brief 'Foreword'. (It would get longer later.)

> The form of the opera is derived from Aristophanes as postulated in F. M. Cornford's 'Origin of Attic Comedy'. The Drowned World is of course the res-mersas of Vergil,[119] while the Heavenly Dance is taken from Sir — 's Orchestra.[120] The Latin title is that of a mediaeval work on alchemy, and the sub-title was suggested to us by Mr E. M. from these lines of T. S. Eliot's 'Burnt Norton':
>
> 'Go, said the bird, for the leaves were full of children,
> Hidden excitedly, containing laughter.'
>
> Other appropriations are too numerous and obvious to need acknowledgement.[121]
>
> D.N.
> M.T.

Francesca Allinson had responded more warmly than John Amis or David Ayerst to the Masque scenario early in 1944. Tippett wrote to his collaborator, 'F. thinks it the goods', and she was also confident that, when the time came, Newton would find the right words to be sung: '[she] thinks you will do it well.' Tippett thought the same. As we have seen, he liked some of Newton's poems very much and urged him to write more, provided they were properly self-expressive:

> What does sound fresh and nice in your stuff is the candour and the candid language that expresses it, and the 'Greek' element is, to my ear, strong and healthy. It also best expresses your own quality.[122]

119 'Res-mersas': *Aeneid* VI. 267. The spelling of 'Vergil' with an 'e' (unusual at that time) is characteristic of W. Jackson Knight. See nn. 191–2 below and associated text.

120 I.e. Sir John Davies, *Orchestra: A Poem of Dancing* (1596). See nn. 194–5 below and associated text. These Virgil and Davies references suggest that draft-lyrics for what would become the big arias in Act I of the eventual opera already existed at this point: texts which, MT stresses (Bowen, *Tippett on Music*, 202), were preceded by musical ideas.

121 Mr E. M.: Edric Maynard; see *C20 Blues*, 121–2. (Maynard also supplied Newton with the epigraph for his 'Rebus': n. 3 above.) 'Go, said the bird…': 'Burnt Norton' I. 40–41.

122 'The goods': BL291.202 (21 Feb 1944). 'What does sound fresh': BL292.16 (11 June 1944).

He was not alone in this admiration. Over the next three or four years, Edith Sitwell would judge that Newton had 'a *real gift* for poetry'; *The Penguin New Writing* under John Lehmann's editorship would publish two short poems of his; *Poetry* (*Chicago*) would publish six in all, and rather later his work would be taken by *Botteghe Oscure* and the *Paris Review*. At one point in 1944 Tippett says that he would like to have

> my copy of whatever you decide to keep. I'm probably useless as a critic of poetical technique etc — but I can see a bit how it goes in general with you and guess what is the next sort of matter to be added to your range.

As a way of widening that range, it seems that Newton was experimenting with larger forms. The same year Tippett enquires 'What is this play you're writing?' and in 1945 he is curious about what he calls Newton's 'Hopkins libretto', though nothing further seems to be known for certain about either of these projects — not even whether the rumoured libretto was tailored for Tippett's friend the composer Antony Hopkins or had as its subject the Victorian priest-poet Gerard Manley Hopkins, whom Newton admired.[123]

Tippett was interested too to read Newton's views on the musical setting of verse, probably as expressed in his essay 'The Composer and the Music of Poetry'. 'All you say of words and music is sound sense,' he writes in January 1944, assuring Newton that in their Masque there would be a distinction between 'musical climaxes' that employed words in one way and 'verbal climaxes' that treated them in another:

> It will be relatively easy because I have constructed it in those terms, i.e. you have spoken and recited argument and drama in I hope a language of simple image[s] which shall 'picture' the thought — then gradually the plane rises or lowers, and the music begins, wherein either the action ceases or the actions alone portray the drama — and so back again to explicit word and image — a rise and fall.

123 'A *real gift* for poetry': BL292.155 (Jan 1946; photocopy in the MT-Newton file of a letter from Sitwell to Newton). 'Whatever you decide to keep': BL291.232 (25 April 1944). 'Play you're writing': BL291.184 (23 Jan 1944): Sch 165. 'Hopkins libretto': BL292.120 (8 July 1945). Admiring G. M. Hopkins: Newton, 'The Composer and the Music of Poetry', 14.

He exchanged ideas with Newton about the sort of instrumental support words should have at particular moments in the plot: for instance in the 'strip-teaze act' soon after Margaret's first entrance when she was to throw off her worldly encumbrances.[124] He relished his collaborator's knowledge of English Renaissance poetry and love for Stravinsky, which enabled composer to urge librettist to mould some of his chorus-texts in the conversational manner of the English madrigal ('each voice should address the other') and some in the hieratic manner of *Oedipus Rex* ('single ideas, arresting words and repetitions').[125] In the early months of their work together he was heartened by the fondness Newton showed for Henry Purcell's contemporary, William Congreve: poet of the English opera *Semele* and the sung masque *The Judgement of Paris*. It was encouraging first because Congreve was a cool yet witty yet weighty versifier with a style that set him apart from what Tippett saw as the self-indulgences of poetic friends of Newton's like young Nick Moore — apart too from Dante-like high solemnity, on the one side, and a overripe Keatsian romanticism, on the other:

> I get the impression (absurd?) that you have a real place (poetic) to stand on between these extremes [...] with your feeling for Congreve. In any case [for] the masque it's no use to go Dante or to go Keats. It wants a limpid clean precise style [...]: gay and witty: to cover the basic lines of the psychological allegory.

It was also encouraging because, as we have seen, it had long been Tippett's idea that the Masque's text should provide words not only for recitatives, arias and choruses but for spoken dialogue too, court-masque-and-*Singspiel*-fashion (with *Die Zauberflöte* ever in the background), and the stylish repartee in Congreve's comedies (*Love for Love, The Way of the World*) would be a sound model for the spoken parts. As late in their partnership as spring 1946 Tippett was stressing that, at one point in the action, the 'moral of the play' needed to be made verbally clear 'in poetry or prose, spoken or sung', and he'd earlier hoped that Newton could pioneer new ways of moving seamlessly *between* speech and song:

124 Words and music: BL291.187 (31 Jan 1944). Strip-teaze: BL291.211 (21 March 1944); for a sketch of the scene—speech, then 'recitative, scena and ensemble'—see First Sketchbook: Add. MS 72054, 8v-9v. (Amused, the chorus of Laughing Children mark Margaret's taking off hat, gloves, cloak, etc. with sung numerals: 'one', 'two', 'three' and so on.)

125 BL292.10 (22 May 1944): Sch 154. (For dating of letter, see n. 105 above).

> I've had an idea about the masque: that whenever the words are to break into recitative, then the last [spoken] couplets must be already in a particular rhythm from which the first notes are struck as if natural. See? [...] Can that be done?[126]

In all, then, Tippett like Allinson was confident that when it came to actual libretto-writing Newton would 'do it well', that he would be able to make speakable and singable sense of all the things he threw at him, albeit with a little guidance perhaps:

> If we can decide on relative timings of things, I think I can take you even further on the necessary road, by listing the ideas, emotions etc, which belong in each chunk of speech, each scene: so that you can say: so many couplets on that matter, so many on this.

That comes from April 1944, and this from the following August:

> I'm thinking I'd better do a fresh précis of the general ideas and associations in my mind behind each conversation, which you can read and discuss before trying to crystallise into a condensed image as suitable: or reject as too complicated or to be left unspoken.[127]

Crystallisation would surely follow. But when? Unlike Nick Moore, Den Newton in his mid-20s was not the fastest or most profuse of writers. Tippett would occasionally chaff at his being so slow, though his slowness where the masque-opera was concerned may have had an understandable element of diffidence in it, a diffidence Tippett did his best to diffuse:

> I don't feel any fears as to your ability to do what is needed — rather more of mine — but I do have anxieties only as to our general lackadaisicalness, and p'raps your own fears of your own attempts; so don't be shy, Den, of anything (please). It's to be a genuine cooperation, which means that we shan't show any script till we've both argued it out and my name is as responsible as yours.

Hence if Newton did send a versified aria-lyric based on a Tippett prose-sketch or a chunk of detailed revised script with timings of scenes, nature of cues and so on—and even more if he sent substantial

126 'Your feeling for Congreve': BL292.83 (14 Nov 1944). 'Spoken or sung': BL292.159 (16 Feb 1946). Words breaking into recitative: BL291.222–3 (16 April 1944).

127 BL291.223 (16 April 1944); BL292.50 (20 Aug 1944): Sch 176.

sections of actual draft-libretto—his composer was overjoyed.[128] Receiving such a draft in 1945 of the scene of George's arrival at the terrain of the Ancients (a draft which, like all Newton's extended efforts, seems not to have survived in its original form), he writes 'I like what's done tremendously — so just go ahead'. Tippett jotted down some detailed comments that supplement the marginal notes and 'pencilled shots' he must have added to the typescript:

> Welcome Chorus: excellent. Gives for a nice modern Purcell Ode start. Isn't there one too many Ancients? — doesn't the rhythm automatically run on — so that it sounds like
>
> Ancient
> A—
> A—
> (Honoured)
> Honoured wardens, etc.
>
> But now — as suddenly re-reading it — I hear it as you've done it. Isn't that stupid? But I'm thinking it's another line is needed between
>
> Honoured etc.
> and
> Maintainers etc.
>
> […] I think the next quatrain is enough — it might be repeatable canon. […] My pencilled shots introduce too many long sounds (words). 'Is not order desirable?' is too quick I feel. I want, sort of, Is not o[rder] — unchangeably desirable? But that's a mouthful. George's sort of language is O.K.; though I fancy it is O.K.-er by us than by others, because we like and appreciate the same sort of play of ideas. It must be a bit obviously pointed perhaps —
>
> For the first time in history —
> I'm going to be married.
>
> Then I want some kind of expostulation, as I've indicated.

(Tippett's allusions to Newton's Welcome Chorus here—'Ancient … 'Honoured' … 'Maintainers'—point pretty directly to some welcoming lines of the Neophytes that survive in the Second Sketchbook:

> Welcome ancient, a —, a —
> honoured guardians of the law

128 'I don't feel any fears…': BL292.119 (3 July 1945). Versified aria-lyric: BL292.102–3 (10 May 1945): Sch 182.

Welcome to the youth also
The disciplined disciples
whose feet tread out the measured path

This bids fair to being the only surviving *Aurora* lyric that we can claim with some certainty as Newton's work, since normally with sketchbook passages it's not possible to be sure whether we have Newton's original drafts transcribed by Tippett or Tippett's revisions/re-workings/replacements of them.)[129]

Remarkably, the operatic sketchbooks and Tippett's letters to Newton contain no musical notation at all and very few verbal indications of musical procedures beyond the unavoidable 'recitative', 'aria', 'trio' and such. Of the five most interesting, two are in that letter about the Welcome Chorus—the 'nice modern Purcell Ode' and the 'repeatable canon'—and the other three we have seen already: the ideas that there should be 'rolls of drums' as King Fisher makes to unveil Sosostris, that the opera's climax should counterpoint a 'ground-bass' dirge over the dead King Fisher with an 'ecstatic coloratura duet' for George and Margaret, and that the work should end with 'a great trill for voices and orchestra'.[130] Still, we've seen that in 1944 Tippett was keeping 'notes of music intended', and it's clear that by 1945 he was thinking about matters of broad 'musical organisation' as well as of text-setting; so his controlling grasp of the whole project may sometimes have made Newton feel sidelined. However, in his letters the composer almost always allows for his librettist's inventive (or at least stylistically refining) input into the project. Thus, when the younger man has their typist send him a new draft for part of Act I, Tippett purrs, if a little nervously:

> It has tremendous possibilities, if it needs a lot of work. [...] The effect of your script on me is to confirm my belief in the work, my confidence in your ability to do the needful, if you could but do it before the few months left run out. [...] What is very pleasing

129 'I like what's done' and 'Welcome Chorus': BL292.172–3 (probably summer/autumn 1945, on account of MT's hopes in the letter that he'll soon 'see the last' of Symphony No. 1, finished in autumn 1945). 'Welcome ancient...': Add. MS 72054, 4v.

130 Further, in the Second Sketchbook (Add MS 72055, 3r) there's a jotting-down of names for several episodes in the planned Act I with a key-signature suggested for each. The key-arrangement (which may well connect with the matters of tonal organisation discussed by Kemp, *Tippett*, 237) is the traditional 'circle of fifths'. Cf. Add MS 72050, 59v, for a further, less systematic page of key-speculations.

> about the script is that the work begins to dramatize itself despite the complicated symbolisms. [...] If I may advise, don't get too entangled in the detail now, but carry through a whole lay-out which we can work at. For, you see, detail *could* be left till I am right in the time of starting. [...] *How* I shall be delighted if *you* really bring it off. Gather yourself together and begin Act 2 and all power to your elbow![131]

Gently keeping Newton moving forward was clearly a priority of Tippett's. As early as spring 1944 he had twice wondered aloud whether his collaborator might have 'a first shot at some of the scenes', presumably in full-fig libretto-mode. ('I wonder if we could risk timing-out 16 scenes now — because if that were done you might find yourself having a shot at one of them.') However, for most of that year there was little sense of urgency over the project, Tippett seeming content that they should go on 'chit-chatting about it till the time to do it finally forces itself on us'. Still, he did hope that there would be a first draft of the libretto by the spring of 1945, partly because, with Britten's *Peter Grimes* coming over the horizon, there was 'going to be a fresh attempt at National Opera, so it's now or never', and partly because he was planning to finish what would become his Symphony No. 1 in the autumn of that year, and wanted at that point to move straight on to the composition of *Aurora Consurgens.* (In the intervening summer months he hoped to circulate a detailed revised scenario-cum-draft-libretto to a wider circle of trusted friends so that it could 'chase around a bit for common criticism': from Edward Dent, Walter Goehr, Arthur Waley, William Glock, Priaulx Rainier and, should he be interested, the stage director Michel Saint-Denis, who was doing such exciting work at the Old Vic Theatre in London.) But then, quite unexpectedly around March 1945, a new string quartet—his Quartet No. 3 in embryo—'suddenly presented itself', rising up and demanding to be written as soon as the Symphony was complete. This put back the urgency of Newton's completing the *Aurora* libretto till the spring 1946; so it was in the winter of 1945–46 that libretto-deadlines became really serious things.[132]

131 BL292.164–5 (? Feb 1946).

132 Having a shot: BL291.198 (15 Feb 1944); BL292.10 (22 May 1944): Sch 154. Chit-chatting: BL291.232 (25 April 1944): Sch 169. First draft and National Opera: BL292.51 (20 Aug 1944): Sch *176. 'For common criticism': MT to Glock, Schuttenhelm, *Selected Letters*, 255. New string quartet: BL292.93.

By then Newton had apparently completed at least a draft of a substantial part of Act I, seemed willing to go on and was still receiving ideas about plotting and staging from Tippett, yet he had slowed to the pace of a snail. The composer had been getting a little impatient and was now worried. 'For heaven's sake,' he wrote early in 1946,

> don't give up now. Can you do Act 2 this spring? I think it will have to be. I must begin laying out the musical pattern at once, more or less — because as the 4tet is now only a matter of months for completion, it's still quite certainly now or never for the opera. How many months do you need for a draft of Act 2? It's rather important to know. I'm still continually frightened that circumstances will trip us up, either by delaying you (who are slow enough as it is!) or by hurrying me — both of which are fairly likely. So I think about 3 more months *at the most* is a sort of date-line. After that I'd have to look around I suppose for a script in a hurry.

In another letter near the same time he tries to explain the nature of the overriding creative complex that has gripped him:

> I have got to the point now, when I am the creature of this complex to a degree which may not be easily observable to a dear friend who is used to personal attention and cherishing. So that, while I *do* have patience with the slowness of my librettist, because he is a dear (where I can't imagine I should have for another and why?), there is an absolute limit beyond friendship when the complex demands action irrespective of whether you have finished it or are in prison. It's not difficult for me now to approach whom I will, but I want it to be by you if you will produce it. [...] [As things now stand] I feel I was a fool, against advice, to turn for collaboration to a friend — because this thing that drives me, that makes me worried now, is so bloody actual, and so *final*. No one in the end can stand in affection against it.[133]

News, probably from John Amis, that Newton had launched into an Act II draft came as temporary balm: 'I can't say how much I'm relieved, [as I] was having nightmares of having to get down to it myself.'

133 MT impatient: see letter to William Glock, Christmas 1945 (Tippett Archive, British Library). 'For Heaven's sake, don't give up': BL292.164. 'I have got to the point': BL292.182–3 (18 Jan 1946): Sch 186–7.

But by early March 1946 nothing (or not much) seems to have been forthcoming from Newton, and on the 13th Tippett felt he had to lay down a kind of ultimatum:

> I do like what you have done (I wish I might have the rest of Act I) but it's no use disguising the circumstantial difficulties — and temperamental ones also! I have got a great deal myself out of your co-operation so far — in ideas and discussion. I must acknowledge that in any case: and handsomely as is appropriate. But I often get the feeling that it were almost better for both of us to leave straining and worrying and let me see what I can do either alone or with help between now and the summer. This indeed would be *easier* for me, if perhaps not a gain for the work itself. If we did decide now to leave it, I have more time to look around. If you decide to go on, then it will become a date-line question: leaving me just enough time, I suppose [should you miss the date-line] to get hold of a quick worker or get myself down to it.[134]

Newton must have indicated not long afterwards that he couldn't fit in with the 'date-line' plan, for by late April Tippett was telling David Webster at Covent Garden: 'It looks as if Den is unlikely to be able to do what I want for the libretto.'[135] It was the end of the collaboration, one protracted perhaps in its last weeks by a solicitous patience of the composer's which, as he said, 'I can't imagine I should have for another and why?' But Tippett was now free to look around for a librettist ('to approach whom I will'), or if need be to 'get down to it myself', nightmares or no nightmares.

134 'I can't say how much': BL292.163 (19 Feb 1946). 'I do like what you have done', and acknowledging handsomely: BL292.166–7 (13 March 1946): Sch 187–8.

135 Schuttenhelm, *Selected Letters*, 311.

6 New directions (Newton *solus*)

Why did Newton pull out? He seems to have left no indication, but there is a lot of evidence to support reasonable speculation in matters personal, inter-personal and career-connected. Personally, for all that he warmed to Tippett in several ways, Newton may have felt that the operatic project was reducing him to the level of a mere syllable-provider for a driven and demanding task-master, to say nothing of committing him to find words for a grand affirmation of the triumph of psychological individuation and related social revolution when privately he was doubtful about such things. In the poems Newton was writing around this time, Jung isn't a strong presence.[136] In one substantial piece, 'Lacking a Guide'—he showed it to Tippett in 1944 (who was intrigued by it) and to Sitwell in 1945 (who was not)—he seems to place himself among

> The dim precursors of the well-assured:
> Failures and refugees,
> The stragglers and the exiles and the lost.

He may have envied the heart's assurance affirmed by Tippett in the opera but had yet to experience it personally; hence a need to find a direction of his own, away from the opera workshop. (Tippett himself had written to him three years before: 'I want you to go your own way and keep your own independence and centre — and to realise and feel full confidence about your own quality.')[137] Then his defaulting

136 A possible exception is the revelatory descent to the lower depths of a Venetian (or Venetian-type) canal in a poem published rather later, in 1954, 'Foundations of Our City'; see Appendix II.

137 'Lacking a Guide': see Appendix II. MT's response to the poem: BL292.40 (2 July 1944). Sitwell's response: BL292.157 (8 Jan 1946). 'Go your own way': BL291.87 (22 April 1943).

may have been for a purely craft-connected reason: one in evidence at the very end of his essay 'The Composer and the Music of Poetry', probably written in 1943–45. There he is led to the assertion that what music needs in the way of words for setting is simple rhythmic speech of the kind to be found in English lyricists from Purcell's time to that of *The Beggar's Opera* or in the songsters of the South Pacific island of Vao, whose music had recently been described by Tippett's friend John Layard in his *Stone Men of Malekula*. 'Words for music', Newton declared,

> should be written [...] with no pretensions to being poetry. Their limits and their capabilities are probably to be found somewhere between the songs of the Vao islanders and those of the English of 1700 — but their ultimate discovery should be the task of another enquiry.[138]

Arguably that enquiry would have resulted in a libretto for *Aurora Consurgens*, but Newton may have found he was too *much* of a poet or, at the age of 25, too self-conscious a one to carry it through.

These things may have inhibited his libretto-writing. Simple fear may have inhibited it as well: a permanent gnawing anxiety late in the War and in the months after it that the men from the Ministry of Labour were planning to lock him up for abandoning farm-work in favour of the London literary life before he had had their permission to do so — something which didn't leave him until the middle of 1946, when he nerved himself to visit the Ministry, only to be told that he was free to *go* free.[139] Then there were inter-personal matters, erotic ones particularly. There had been a brief flirtation with a nameless girl in 1943 which Tippett, hearing about it from a mutual friend and determined that there'd never be 'triangular problems' in his relationship with Newton, had been quick to approve:

> Bryan [Fisher] told me you have met along with a girl special to yourself — which sounds very good. Though I don't think you have the elaborate beauty which the poet deemed Mr W. H. to have, I've no doubt you'll be as worthy of being urged to repeat yourself sooner or later.

138 'The Composer and the Music of Poetry', 20. Songs of Vao: Layard, *Stone Men of Malekula* (London, 1942), 284–5, 404 and 636–9.

139 Settle, *Learning to Fly*, 155. Newton and prison: Schuttenhelm, *Selected Letters*, 255.

Newton himself recalls the affair wryly but fondly in a poem published in 1947, 'Onionskin Man', seeing it as forming one of the layers of his Peer Gynt-like personality.[140] But more seriously and momentously, at an At Home of his Cambridge/LSE patron Lance Beales, probably early in 1944, he met the young American we have heard from twice already: she who evoked the Cambridge Conchies so sympathetically and who saw Newton himself as 'the best-read person I have ever known'. This was the intelligent and articulate future novelist Mary Lee Settle, two years Newton's senior, married with a very young son, estranged from her husband, serving in the U.K. Women's Air Force in Herefordshire and Wiltshire and then at the U.S. Army War Information Office in London. She and Newton were evidently attracted to each other. Tippett was philosophical about it, writing to Allinson in May 1944:

> Den [is] such a nice lad — and growing now at such a pace. I fancy that he's taken a sudden jerk on again and that the need for physical warmth which he had of me is passing. [...] Luckily for me I [...] have always known that the pace of the friendship has to be set by the younger person, and that in his case in the long run it's the intellectual stimulus he really wants

— though Tippett's need for physical warmth from Den was still being answered in August that year:

> I suppose it's a weakness and imposition to want to be sometimes in your arms, and you're wonderfully gentle and good about it. [...] Because it's you, the pleasure is pure and unmixed and I lie on happy as a child.[141]

It seems that it wasn't until the late summer of 1945, when the European War at least was well over and Mary Lee had been back to America, divorced her husband, collected her son Christopher from his grandparents and returned to Britain (preferring London's fatigued resilience to the rich smugness of New York), that she and Newton really

140 'Triangular problems': BL292.14 (7 June 1944). 'Bryan told me': BL291.120 (17 Sept 1943). For 'Onionskin Man', see Appendix II. For 'Mr W. H.' and fatherhood, see Shakespeare, *Sonnets* 1–17.

141 Settle's War: see *All the Brave Promises*, *passim*, and Chs. 6 and 7 of *Learning to Fly*. MT philosophical: letter to Allinson of 4 May 1944, Schuttenhelm, *Selected Letters*, 113. MT's weakness, Den's gentleness: BL292.45 (16 Aug 1944): Sch 174.

and fully came together. One of their first meetings after her arrival back in London was at a Wigmore Hall concert. At first she had declined Newton's invitation to go, but at the last minute she changed her mind impulsively and arrived to find not only Den there but 'Michael Tippett, one of England's leading young composers'. After the concert, she writes, the three of them 'walked down Wigmore Street on the way to an Indian restaurant. [...] Michael was wearing my white gloves over his ears and Den was wearing my hat.'[142]

Late in 1945 Den and Mary Lee were moving towards marriage, and in 1946 married they were. The exhilaration of the approach of this and the practicalities involved, which of course included Newton's becoming a stepfather (and a good one too, apparently), may not have allowed much time for, or concentration on, libretto-writing. Tippett had to face this: 'Sometimes now I can't help feeling that the new happiness is of more importance than the libretto, to you, at present.'[143] Worrying though this was, he nonetheless refused to belittle or criticise Newton's feelings. The anxious January letter in which he berates himself for being 'a fool, against advice, to turn for collaboration to a friend' still finishes with warm sympathy and an allusion to Blake's 'He who kisses the Joy as it flies/Lives in Eternity's sunrise':

> Best of love, poppet, and I'm terribly pleased for you that you are having the experience you are; and may it be a true 'joy as it flies' / dein treuester Freund / Michael.

Again, the March letter which includes the 'date-line' ultimatum that effectively brought the collaboration to an end begins with the neighbourly and domestic 'Herewith two tickets for the "Child" on Tuesday. [...] If Mary can't go because of Christopher, take Priaulx or someone on the spare.' *Chez* the newly-wed Newtons, things would sometimes be domestic literally. 'Michael Tippett often stayed with us', Mary Lee later recalled. 'One morning he came into the kitchen and announced that he had had the best night's sleep since leaving the Scrubs.'[144]

On the back of the envelope of the January 1946 letter ending with that Blake quotation, Tippett wrote 'If you'd rather leave [the opera] at this stage for your own work, I should quite understand' — which leads to the more public possible reason for Newton's pulling out of

142 Settle, *Learning to Fly*, 142–3; see Ch. 8 for Settle in 1944–45.

143 BL292.166 (13 March 1946): Sch 187. Newton as stepfather: Settle, *Learning to Fly*, 154–7.

144 Settle, *Learning to Fly*, 155.

the collaboration. During the War and its aftermath, the composer had had wise words for his librettist about the problems and opportunities of combining an artistic vocation with a job that yielded a living wage and perhaps helped to underpin a marriage too. While working in the Cambridgeshire fields Newton had flirted with the idea of staying on in farming: he had developed a liking and respect for it. ('Being a farmer is more important than being an artist,' he would later declare to the high-cultured readers of the *New English Weekly*.)[145] But a part-time career in some corner of the arts came to be more appealing. Tippett had some tentative suggestions, but in the end it was Lance Beales who came up with a more attractive notion.

In the autumn of 1944 Beales had joined the editorial board of a new publishing venture, Contact Publications, masterminded by the young George Weidenfeld. Its aim, once the War was over, was to publish *Contact*: a series of miscellany volumes, two or three a year, designed and crafted in the most up-to-date way ('brilliant and bizarre', Weidenfeld called it), each volume focussing loosely on a single social or cultural issue. Beales seems to have used his influence on his protégé's behalf, and Newton soon found himself one of the team setting the project up. Riskily where his Conchie status was concerned (as we have seen), he moved from Cambridge to London in the spring of 1945 to help prepare *Contact*'s early numbers, acting as advertising-copy writer, pictorial researcher and 'assistant at large' for various early volumes and as Assistant Editor for the third ('Points of Contact').[146]

At first Tippett approved. In November 1944 he had endorsed the Beales plan and happily passed on what he'd heard was the view of the rising young painter and Morley College concert-regular, John Craxton: that one of Newton's tasks would be 'to mediate between painters, poets and musicians so that we make the rounded society

145 Wise words: BL291.124-5 (28 Sept 1943): Sch 155-6; BL292.184-5 (17 June 1945): Sch 184–5. Farming: 'The Artist's Responsibility', *New English Weekly*, 28/3, Nov. 1945, 25–6.

146 For Beales and Weidenfeld, see Ch. 6 ('The Birth of Contact') in G. Weidenfeld, *Remembering My Friends: An Autobiography* (London, 1995), 115–38, esp. 119–20 and 127–8. Later, Newton would contribute brief articles on fabric- and furniture-design to a magazine with an equally brilliant and bizarre layout, *The Architectural Review*; see under 1952 in his Bibliography (Appendix II) below. In the early 1950s, he also contributed close on 30 book-reviews to *Time and Tide*; see under 1952–56 in his Bibliography. Notably he praised Beckett's *Watt* there before its author had achieved his first British fame with the English *Godot* (Vol. 35, p. 56) and Dylan Thomas's *Under Milk Wood*, as printed in part in *Botteghe Oscure*, before the BBC memorably broadcast it (Vol. 33, p. 856).

we need'. From 1945 to 1947 Newton was also involved with the *New English Weekly*, writing several pieces for it, including his celebrations of Henry Miller and Paul Goodman. He had been recruited to the *Weekly* by his good Conchie friend Patrick Heron, Patrick being the son of Thomas Milner Heron who was close to Philip Mairet, the paper's editor, and sat on its editorial committee. (Patrick and Den made their debuts in the *Weekly*, as art critic and cultural commentator respectively, within a fortnight of each other, and there was even one issue, on 10 January 1946, when their columns—on Picasso, on Sophocles—appeared back-to-back.)[147] By June 1945, a month after Victory in Europe, Tippett was coming to think that the *Weekly* was a safer prospect for Newton than *Contact*, which at that point seems to have been having teething troubles:

> I have an idea that the Contact goings-on may appear a bit worse because everyone is a trifle emotionally deflated by the peace. [...] [However,] Contact asks too much I guess and so will eventually break down. But New Eng Weekly will hope for a loyalty of 2 or 3 years at least.[148]

One way and another, Newton was becoming a writer-about-London, and it could well have been his 'own work', combined with some or all of those other factors ideological and familial, that brought his collaboration with Tippett to an end. True, a lot of that work was in straightforward prose, but he *was* still writing poems until at least the mid-1950s, the major 'late' achievement being the lengthy verse + prose dialogue for two voices, *Lights with Us*, which has echoes of Shaw, Yeats and Auden, and which sets the prophet Tiresias and the newly blinded and exiled King Oedipus at one another's throats. *Lights with Us* is doubly intriguing in relation to *Aurora Consurgens*: first in that it is a debate between Seer and Man of Action, so harking back to the exchanges in *Aurora* drafts between Sosostris and King Fisher; second in that it includes a couple of inset lyrics which suggest that Newton

147 MT's endorsement and Craxton: BL292.78 (8 Nov 1944). (Cf. Newton in 'The Artist's Responsibility' [n. 145 above]: 'An artist is not a politician or a prophet. He is not the storm; he is like a barometer hinting at the climate of the future and reflecting his age.') Miller and Goodman essays: see n. 63 above. For Patrick Heron's manoeuvres to get Newton into the *New English Weekly*'s stable of regulars, see his letters to Newton of 4 Jan and 3 Sept 1944: Douglas Newton Archive © 2017 Virginia-Lee Webb PhD, Box 3 (All Rights Reserved).

148 BL292.109 (17 June 1945).

had found an effective libretto-manner — for instance, in these quatrains from the ballad given to Oedipus as he recalls his initially happy reign over Thebes after the defeat of the Sphinx:

> There lies the city,
> laughing, white with joy;
> awake from nightmare,
> death is lost at last. [...]
>
> In fields, the dancers,
> arms above their heads,
> rise and bow and sink
> slow as corn.[149]

One positive aspect of the end of the collaboration with Tippett is that there's nothing to suggest there was any bad feeling between the two men as a result of it, though it seems that by degrees they came to see less and less of each other. Newton flew the Tippett flag in public on at least one occasion after that end. When a shortened version of *A Child of Our Time* was given at one of Robert Meyer's Children's Concerts in March 1948, Newton wrote a 1,200-word introductory piece about the composer in general and his oratorio in particular for Meyer's associated 'Magazine Devoted to Young Concert-Goers', *Crescendo*. It's an affectionate and perceptive piece which allows itself to reveal (without going into details) that Tippett 'is now at work on an opera which has occupied his thoughts for many years.'[150] It's possible too that Newton more personally and knowingly saluted the operatic project around this time, though if so it was in a cryptic way. In 1947 his poem 'The Annunciation to the Virgin', an evocation of the Archangel Gabriel kneeling before Mary at sunset, appeared on its own in a limited pamphlet edition. At that stage it had no inscription or dedication, but six years later the poet included it in his slim selection of his own poems, *Metamorphoses of Violence*, and there it was inscribed 'In Honour of Claudio Monteverdi'.[151] The Annunciation, then, was to be seen and heard as celebrated in Monteverdi's *Vespro della Beata*

149 *Lights with Us: A Dialogue*, in *Botteghe Oscure* 15 (1955), 163–99. Oedipus' ballad: pp. 175–80. The dialogue's climactic moment of understanding (p. 197)—'I am the only home I know / I am the rock on which I build'—looks forward to MT's epigraph from *All's Well that Ends Well* for *The Knot Garden*: 'Simply the thing I am shall make me live.'

150 Newton, 'Michael Tippett', *Crescendo* 14 (March 1948), 5–7 and 13.

151 See Appendix II below.

Virgine of 1610: a work whose belated first British performance—by Morley College forces conducted by Walter Goehr in 1946—had had Tippett as its moving spirit (and as the composer of an organ prelude for the work).[152] The poem's climax comes as

> a fiery line along the air
> traces the verge of Gabriel's wings
> as light meanders on a lake
> and clearly as angel sings: [...]
> *Mary, Mary, Mary, Mary.*

— a reminiscence, surely, of the *Vespro*'s 'Audi coelum', that remarkable echo-motet (the text in part deriving from the *Song of Solomon*) with its awed repetitions of 'Maria, Maria, Maria, Maria'. And how does the motet describe the Blessed Virgin a few lines before? As one 'who glitters like the rising dawn' — 'quae *consurgens* ut *aurora* rutilat'...

152 See Robinson, *Michael Tippett: Music and Literature*, 134–5, 158–61.

7 Fresh beginnings and continuities (Tippett *solus*)

By the late spring of 1946, Tippett himself was alone with his opera. To judge from his earlier letters to Newton, his first impulse would have been to 'look around [...] for a script in a hurry', to 'get hold of a quick worker', as it was imperative that he should begin composing that autumn and as it was 'not difficult for me now to approach whom I will' — the 'now' presumably reflecting the success in 1944 of the première of *A Child of Our Time*. But whom to approach? Three names suggest themselves: Ronald Duncan, George Barker and Christopher Fry, each a poet with an interest in drama, each roughly Tippett's age or a few years younger, each pacifist or near-pacifist and each a friend or professional protégé of T. S. Eliot's. With Ronald Duncan, there is evidence in the poet's memoirs that Tippett did approach him around the time that things were getting problematical with Newton about a project which may have been *Aurora Consurgens*. It was not long after the successful run of Duncan's 'masque' and 'antimasque' on the life of Saint Anthony, *This Way to the Tomb*, with its incidental score by Benjamin Britten. This had opened in November 1945:

> I had a letter from Michael Tippett asking me to meet him at Fullers tea shop at Victoria. He wanted me to write a libretto for him and suggested a Masque in similar form to *This Way to the Tomb*. Over more buttered toast we discussed a possible theme: unlike Ben, whose mind was always kept to simple dramatic elements without intellectual overlay, Tippett rushed to see a metaphysical or symbolical connotation everywhere. We sketched out a possible subject which he became more and more enthusiastic about as he perceived more complexities in it.[153]

153 Duncan, *How to Make Enemies* (London, 1968), 55. MT seems never to have considered Eliot himself as a collaborator: cf. Schuttenhelm, *Selected Letters*, 60, 61.

However, Duncan had to tell Tippett that he was deep in work on the libretto for Britten's *Rape of Lucretia* at the time—it would open in July—and so was not free to pursue the scheme any time soon.

George Barker may also have seemed attractive. Tippett had come close to collaborating with him in 1937–38 over an ambitious projected choral work, *Nekyia.* It had come to nothing, but they met again in 1943 when the poet was fresh back from quite a long stay in New York. (Tippett quizzed him then about Paul Goodman whom Barker had met there, passing on his account of the American to Newton.) Though Barker in 1946 hadn't as yet had a play performed, he did have strong dramatic interests; but even if Tippett had asked him, he would not have been able to produce a text over that summer, as he would be spending three fraught months back in America at the time.[154] (This hypothetical invitation and refusal would be mirrored by an actual event about ten years later, when Tippett, through pressure of work, had to refuse the BBC's request for music for one of Barker's radio plays, his morality *The Seraphina.*)[155]

Perhaps, then, the third of our poet-pacifists might oblige. Tippett had worked with Christopher Fry closely and amicably on various projects in the 1920s and 1930s, and they were to have further productive times in the 1950s and beyond.[156] So, why not in the 1940s too? True, from 1940 to 1945 (years when there was only very slight contact between them), [157] Fry was otherwise occupied: serving as a hard-pressed member of the Non-Combatant Corps at various sites of German bombing around Britain; having double pneumonia and a breakdown as a result; recovering and directing a certain amount of theatre in Oxford; and, hidden away in the Cotswolds, writing his wittily outrageous career-establishing comedy, *A Phoenix too Frequent.* However, with the War over and *Phoenix* behind him—it was premièred in the spring of 1946—Fry could quite possibly have met up with Tippett at some teashop near a London terminus and talked about future plans, operas perhaps among them. Yet he would surely have pointed out very quickly (if his old colleague needed to be told)

154 Collaboration in the 1930s: see Soden, *Michael Tippett*, 194–6. Barker meeting Goodman: BL291.176 (5 Jan 1944). For Barker from 1943 to 1946, see R. Fraser, *The Chameleon Poet: A Life of George Barker* (London, 2001), Chs. 22–6.

155 Schuttenhelm, *Selected Letters*, 16.

156 O. Soden, 'The Clarion Airs of Michael Tippett and Christopher Fry', *Musical Quarterly*, 97/4 (2014), 616–60.

157 They may have met at Nottingham in spring 1944, when MT had 'a letter out of the blue' from Fry: BL291.222 (16 April 1944).

that, for all the fast-moving ease and vivacity of his stage-dialogue in *Phoenix*, he was an extremely slow worker, so that a summer 1946 deadline would be impossible.[158] Besides, the actor-manager Alec Clunes was dangling a proposition in front of him that he should be Staff Dramatist at Clunes's Arts Theatre, which would require/enable him to spend all his creative time writing a full-length West End play. (It would become his big hit, *The Lady's Not for Burning*.) So again, no dice.

Still, the composer seems to have kept open the possibility of some kind of collaboration until at least late April 1946, while allowing too that he might have to go it alone: 'I *may* have to make the first attempt myself,' he told David Webster. But soon his 'nightmares' came true with the realisation that he *would* have to 'get myself down to it' and write his own libretto. He had done it with *Child of Our Time* after all, and it did have one advantage. He could contrive to keep the text verbally plain and economical, so avoiding the vice his opera might well have fallen into if he had got any of our three poets to contribute to it: the vice of giving words too high a profile. This he thought a major failing of the Duncan-Britten *Rape of Lucretia* when he saw it later in 1946. Though he admired the piece in several ways, he felt bound to remind the composer after the event that the responsibility of a libretto was

> to present emotions and characters in terms of dramatic situation and gesture where the words they actually sing withdraw a bit into the background. Arthur Waley wrote me a letter a little while back [after he and Tippett had seen a performance of Donizetti's *Don Pasquale*] in which he gave his ideal of a libretto: 'one which we are not aware of, so that we come out of the theatre and say later "I suppose there *was* a libretto".'[159]

Tippett agreed with Waley, and duly went ahead to make the libretto himself.

His going it alone was to lead to an opera about which several writers, wholly and quite properly focussed on its achieved text and score as fixed things, have given us valuable essays, studies and

158 For Fry's career 1939–45, see D. Stanford, *Christopher Fry Album* (London, 1952), 16–22, 37–8. Slow worker: Fry, *An Experience of Critics* (London, 1952), 23–4.

159 'Make the first attempt': Schuttenhelm, *Selected Letters*, 311 (letter of 29 April 1946: emphasis mine). 'To present emotions': Schuttenhelm, *Selected Letters*, 199. Cf. Kemp, *Tippett*, 212.

commentaries.[160] There's no call to attempt another such here, and it's not my concern to do so. However, given that Process *is* my concern—the work and its attendant collaboration as developing things—it might be worth suggesting just how much continuity there is in scenario-and-idea matters between the Tippett-Newton *Aurora Consurgens* of 1943–46 and the Tippett-*solus* opera that followed; this partly to lay down a path to Chapter III of Eric Walter White's *Tippett and His Operas*, which throws light on the development of *Midsummer Marriage* from 1948 to its completion in 1952, and partly to give proper emphasis and celebration to the wartime conversations with Newton and the draftings by him that Tippett so valued at the time.

To stress the continuities is not to deny that there were major differences between the 1943–46 and 1946–52 projects: four of them especially. One was in naming. As White chronicles, Tippett became unhappy with the names of his 'plighted pair', Margaret and George, eventually making them the more Celtic Jenifer (in the late 1940s) and Mark (around 1950); and his publisher's manager recoiled from the piece's having a Latin title that derived—of all things—from medieval alchemy. Rather, let the title be in English, let it be explicitly marital and let it signal clearly that the action no longer takes place in the 'eternal spring' of the original Masque-concept but during a Midsummer celebration that could incorporate a climactic St John's Eve fire ceremony. (It is in 1948 that Tippett's published correspondence refers to the piece as *The Midsummer Marriage* for the first time.)[161] Second and crucially important, there was the *Marriage*'s musical texture, which was no longer to be that of a *Singspiel* with spoken episodes interspersing the dances and sung numbers (still the intention up to spring 1946, as we have seen)[162] but that of a quasi-Grand Opera with no speech and almost continuous orchestral sound. Possibly this was an acknowledgment on Tippett's part that it was not within his verbal range to write the kind of crisp, witty linking Congrevian dialogue he had hoped Newton would produce for their *Singspiel*-type Masque; but more likely it was the fruit, at least in part, of his intuition that

160 See Preface above and Select Bibliography below.

161 Changing names: White, *Tippett*, 59–62. Changing title: *C20 Blues*, 216. Title's earliest appearance in letters: White, *Tippett*, 48; cf. *Radio Times* of 7.5.1948, p. 17. Original spring setting: see above, nn. 36 and 102. (White's witness in these matters is valuable, though one should treat very sceptically his assertion, p. 46, that from 1944 on 'there was no doubt in Tippett's mind. He would write the libretto himself.')

162 See above, n. 126 ('spoken or sung').

there was something 'symphony'-like about Cornford's concept of the structure of the Greek texts that he and Newton had been considering in connection with the shaping of their own text: something that, if given its head, would lead to the *Marriage* becoming—texturally if not textually—less *Zauberflöte* and more *Frau ohne Schatten*. (Edward Sackville-West had introduced Tippett to Strauss's opera in 1945, describing it as 'a miracle of getting every conceivable and inconceivable stage-action embedded in a web of music.')[163]

Third, and almost as important, was the decision sometime in 1946, after the collaboration had foundered, to have the mysterious Neophytes of the hilltop temple represented solely by a dance-troupe and to give the opera's chorus (also Neophytes heretofore) a new role. As Tippett told Newton—a friend still though no longer a colleague—that summer,

> I've had some funny and also disquieting times with [the opera;] a few days ago, it grew a 3rd act [= between the earlier scenario's first and second]. But [...] the most radical change is that the choir is [now] a group of George's young friends given an early morning assignation at 'the place'. [...] The play between the humans and their mythological projections gives a new dramatic 'tool of the trade', which clarifies things a bit and makes them less arbitrary.

It may well have been around the time of the arrival of this new type of wholly human 'choir' that he added a paragraph to that brief Foreword drafted in the First Sketchbook, declaring that

> the opera is never purely naturalistic, though it begins as that, nor merely abstract. There is a transition from the time where the natural people are quite distinct from the supernatural (as at the beginning) to the two agonic moments [late in Acts I and III] when they are unified. In these agon(s) the whole stage action is as though it was the vision of the singing chorus, being imagined by themselves and presented to the spectators for comment.[164]

163 BL292.172.

164 'Funny and disquieting times': BL292.115: Sch 183. (Schuttenhelm dates this letter June 1945 while the BL is more hesitant; but the reference near the beginning of it to MT's Third String Quartet points to the summer of 1946.) 'Never fully naturalistic': Add. MS 72054, 3v. (MT seems to have developed the draft foreword to the libretto still further in the late 1940s, but then had second thoughts as to whether such a thing *should* be 'printed with the text for ever'—White, *Tippett*, 59—and dropped it.)

The difference in style between the old *Aurora* masque-chorus and the new *Marriage* opera-chorus is clear early in a transitional draft in which both appear. In the old mode we have a vocal onstage-audience of inquisitive Neophytes:

CHORUS: We are th'eternal spectators of the play.
Ancient masters of the ceremonies,
What have you fresh for us to see today?
ANCIENTS: Why should you always crave for something new?
CHORUS 1: There is to be a marriage, we believe:
King Fisher's daughter and the orphan George.
But the father refuses his consent.
CHORUS 2: What is remarkable in that?
BOTH: Let us first prelude the morning with
Our ritual dance

— and in the new mode we have a crowd of 'George's young friends':

HALF-CHORUS: This way! This way!
Don't go too far down there
But keep the path together.
MEN: Ah — here's a sort of clearing.
Is this the place he meant d'you think?
WOMEN: I hope it gets a little lighter.
Anything might happen here.[165]

Something like naturalism (for a while at least) replaces the earlier *Lehrstück* manner, which allows a role-mutation for the Ancients from the teachers/presenters/masters-of-ceremonies of the earlier concept—half-in and half-out of the drama—to the sage priest-like characters almost wholly within the story of the opera as we know it. There's also, in 'Is this the place *he* meant?', the beginning of a feeling of concentration on George-later-Mark, so that, in the fourth of the major changes, the opera becomes predominantly his and Margaret-later-Jenifer's, where the Masque (though it gave the 'plighted pair' a special prominence) had been more truly the eight-some reel that Tippett in 1943 had called a 'general dance': a reel that lead to what in 1944 he called a 'general marriage'. This change can be seen clearly in the evolution from the mid-1940s to the early 1950s of the closing scene. In the 1944 scenario, after the transfigured couple

165 Third Sketchbook, Add. MS 72056, 4r and 8r.

have returned to the everyday world, Jack and Bella, playing Doctor and Nurse as part of what Tippett in a letter calls 'the George and Dragon mummery', bring King Fisher magically back to a kind of shadow-life in time for the finale, propping him up 'with his paper crown and sceptre'.[166] However, a later account of this scene in one of the sketchbooks has George (as he still was) asking the Ancients if they would resurrect the King and receiving the reply:

> No. His pride undid him.
> Mourn him not. Live at peace together.
> Kingfisher's gross material pride of power
> falls to self-destruction.[167]

Another sketchbook entry, later still (*circa* 1950, the plighted pair now being Mark and Jenifer), envisages something like a traditional final 'walk-down' of five of the principals as the mist clears after the final ritual scene and dawn begins to come up:

> Issuing from the birdsong Strephon's flute is heard, and Strephon himself appears out of the mist, dancing down to the edge of the steps that lead to the lower stage, calling with his flute to each side. Jack leads on M[ark] left and Bella leads on J[enifer] right.

'Now', Jack and Bella sing, 'the weddings [NB the plural] can take place at last', and the She-Ancient appears with a pitcher of wine.[168] But by 1952, not only has King Fisher been definitively and quite terminally carried off in funeral cortège, but Jack and Bella have long since eloped and Strephon has withdrawn with the Ancients into the temple. Only Mark and Jenifer are left onstage with their good friends the chorus, before, in a final nod to Cornford's Aristophanes, a general *exeunt* leaves the dawn-lit hilltop unpeopled for the orchestral epilogue.[169]

That's all very true and important. Yes, there were striking changes. Nonetheless, the continuity between *Aurora Consurgens* and

166 'General dance': see text at n. 60 above; 'general marriage': text at n. 105. 'Mummery': BL292.160 (16 Feb 1946).

167 Third Sketchbook: Add. MSS 72056, 69r, 70r.

168 Strephon's flute: Sixth Sketchbook, Add. MS 72059, 38r–v. 'Now the weddings…' and wine: Third Sketchbook, Add. MS 72056.

169 Elopement: It was not until spring 1951 that MT decided that Jack and Bella were '*not* returning' for the finale (White, *Tippett*, 67). Cornford's Aristophanes: *Origin*, 8.

The Midsummer Marriage is just as striking, and not only in the obvious ways where much of the outer plot and several of the character-relationships are concerned. There are subtler connections too. Several things that appear new in the later opera can, if one looks closely, be seen to grow out of matters that Newton and Tippett were discussing and planning from 1943 to 1946, or to emerge from books Tippett had been reading in earlier years.

The most obvious disjunction between *Aurora* and the *Marriage* on a plot-level involves the discarding of the mooted central episode of fetching the barrel and revealing its contents. Tippett had presumably come to feel that his symbolic barrel's analogies with intelligent Celtic cauldrons and ancient treasure-containers were too obscure to work in the opera house, that his net's resonances with Babylonian *logos*-mystics and with his beloved Goethe were too private and that—Greek shark-priests or no Greek shark-priests—the sharp-toothed fish's correspondence with the *penis dentatus* of his dream was too acutely personal. The old symbolisms would have to be discarded and new, more legible ones found.[170] But although big changes were indeed made to the opera's central symbols between 1946 and 1952, the change in what was *being* symbolised was much smaller, and the materials from which the new symbols were made had very largely been to hand for some time.

'There is no barrel of sea-water,' Tippett wrote laconically to Newton in that letter of summer 1946. What, then, could replace Jack's being nipped by a significant sea-creature and scurrying into Bella's comforting arms? Well, perhaps one could—adding a Shavian strain to the Darwinian—reverse the sexes and give a similar crisis and response to Bella herself. It's an idea that seems to have appealed to Tippett, and after some experiments in interfacing natural and supernatural scenes—Eric Walter White encouraging and assisting—the two men came on a way to make it work. Bella, who has just made a leap-year proposal of marriage to Jack, witnesses the climax of a sequence of ritualised enactments by the Neophyte dancers of animal pursuit and near-capture, the female being the pursuer in each case. She is affected profoundly by this animal-pantomime—as dream perhaps, or as vision, certainly as forced acknowledgment of ancient primal impulse—but, once Jack has calmed her a little,

170 In the late 1940s MT showed Eric Walter White a draft scenario-script for the opera but said that White should ignore 'earlier discarded symbolisms [in it] — e.g. nets and fishing.' White, *Tippett*, 55.

she responds to it with an affirmation of civilised, up-to-date female identity, putting on the necessary mask of stylish make-up and attractively adjusted hair. Tippett was happy to have Bella's proposal scene—her catching of Jack, so to speak—placed in apposition to the animal-dances in this way, telling White that it 'fits nicely with the hunting of Strephon'.[171]

And the net which Strephon had drawn out of the barrel in the 1944 scenario? It had had the intelligence to entangle the dangerous King Fisher and then embrace the reunited George and Margaret up to the moment in the Masque when, in one sketch for the scene by Newton or Tippett, the Ancients signalled that the revels they had been presenting would soon be ended:

> Children, unhang the magic net
> That knits and knots mankind together.
> Collect within it the precious pair
> Of golden fishes. So the vision
> Cease, the drama end.[172]

The net as central symbol is set aside. In its place at the climax there are veils, gauzes and eventually giant lotus petals, all growing out of the relatively simple Sosostris-construct of the 1944 scenario: that splendid piece of theatrical machinery which would have been the envy of the devisers of any seventeenth-century court masque.[173] What was new in the re-thinking of the construct in the late 1940s was that the veils, waving 'in fantastic shapes and swirls in a surrounding night', were to gain powers of metamorphosis and that magic fire would be involved, though for several months Tippett was not sure just how these powers were to be used. As late as 1949 he was writing to Eric Walter White, 'the matter of the Fire Dance and its relationship to the rest,

171 Bella dreaming: MT suggests in his plot-summary of the completed opera (Fifth Sketchbook) that the dances are 'perhaps' Bella's dreams. Scene fitting nicely: White, *Tippett*, 55. For the origins of the Ritual Dances, see Section VIII below.

172 Third Sketchbook: Add. MS 72056, 66v. 'Pair' was originally 'catch', which was first emended to 'draft' and only then to 'pair'; 'drama' was an emendation of 'ritual'. Cf. Eisler, *Orpheus the Fisher*, 262–3.

173 Cf., e.g., the 'high vast obelisk' in Thomas Campion's *Lords' Masque* (1613) which the 'reverend dame', the prophetess Sybilla, 'did draw [...] forth with a thread of gold' onto the stage of the Whitehall Banqueting House. It was 'all of silver, and in it lights of several colours', being 'of that height, that the top thereof touched the highest clouds.' T. Spencer *et al.*, eds, *A Book of Masques* (Cambridge, 1967), 115.

and to the "reconciling symbol", the visionary transcendence — and the veils and Strephon. There's still a tie-up which eludes us.'[174]

His first thoughts about the veils and their setting-off the transfigured, mystically married couple they have within them can be found in the Sixth Sketchbook. This includes a draft 'script' which for a while is quite close in action and ideas to what would become the opera's Act III in its final form. So Sosostris envisions the lovers' union and King Fisher, outraged, profanely unveils her (the veils being taken up by the chorus), at which the lovers magically appear in the vanishing Sosostris's place and the King is felled. But as Strephon makes fire for the final dance, Sketchbook Six goes its own way:

> With the lifted stick Str[ephon] lights the mens' torches, so that there is that much more light on the stage besides the radiance of the transfiguration. The other dancers take the veils from the girls of the Chorus and begin a dance with them, a dance which may bear some relation to the stiffer net dance of the opening scene[175] but whose object is eventually to re-veil the transfiguration. They do this in such a way that finally Mark and Jenifer are enclosed as within the shell of a black almond, but still visible because the shell exactly in front of them is left open.

The lovers sing together: 'The world is formed/made/shaped by our desire...' and Strephon and the dancers take the torches from the chorus men. 'Strephon sets fire to the pile of veils by leaping into the black almond, closing therebye the last gap.'[176]

174 Elusive tie-up: White, *Tippett*, 58. 'Fantastic shapes': MT to E. Sackville-West, Schuttenhelm, *Selected Letters*, 283. When MT evokes his concept of Sosostris for Barbara Hepworth (*Selected Letters*, 355), it is as 'the Pythia on the tripod'; and perhaps the image of the Greek oracle high and lifted up on her three-legged stool lies behind Sosostris's mighty triangular-conical form: a likelihood increased by the fact that the tranced, visionary climactic speech of Mrs George Collins in Shaw's *Getting Married*, a speech much admired by MT—BL292.159 (16 February 1946)—is described by one of its hearers as 'the convulsions of the pythoness on the tripod'.

175 As described in the Sixth Sketchbook, 7r-8r, the party-scene at the beginning of Act III had included a Goethe-inflected net-dance: 'A girl holds the end of a ribbon, which she pays out or pulls in at need. On the stage below, 5 other girls have woven the ribbon into a kind of net in which they have caught 5 boys who with knives or scissors continually try to get free. Every so often one of them does so by cutting the ribbon but as quickly he is caught again and the ribbon knotted.'

176 BL Add. MS 72059, 32r, 33r, 34r.

The 'almond' is the time-honoured 'mandorla': a frame made up of two arcs (created by overlapping a pair of circles) which has seen service in various symbolisms but notably in that of medieval Christianity. However, the mandorla didn't fully serve Tippett's turn, perhaps for practical reasons—it would certainly have been very difficult to stage—or perhaps because as a stage-image it might seem to sail dangerously close to blasphemy to a Christian audience or conversely might, as Strephon steps inside it, stir grim memories of Druidic burning-alive ceremonies at pagan Celtic fire-festivals: the kinds of 'wicker man' event Frazer describes chillingly at the end of the chapter 'Balder's Fires' in *The Golden Bough*. Whichever the reason, Tippett's thoughts about this episode turned from mandorlas to mandalas.

Image 7.1 Mandorla of the Virgin and Child: detail from Carlo Crivelli, *The Vision of the Blessed Gabriele; © The National Gallery, London.*

His re-thinking of the scene seems to have been stimulated by his looking again at his cherished Taoist *Secret of the Golden Flower* as presented to the West by Wilhelm and Jung. As we have seen, George/Mark and Margaret/Jenifer can be read as embodiments of the *I Ching* trigrams *K'an* (*Eros*-water-moon) and *Li* (*Logos*-light-sun), and a commentary on the *Secret* quoted by Wilhelm asserts that when *K'an* and *Li* unite, 'the Golden Flower appears.' (Wilhelm also sets up a diagram of movement from the mystic *Tao* to the blooming of the Flower *via* the separation and ultimate reunion of the complimentary lines of *Yin*–femininity–*Eros*–life–darkness–Anima and *Yang*–masculinity–*Logos*–essence–light–Animus; and Mark and Jenifer's progress from first love to love transfigured involves the same concepts, if with rather more twists and turns *en route*.) Jung's commentary connects the Flower with the painting and sometimes also the dancing of mandalas: those harmonious circular figures, sometimes lotus-based, that are expressive of cosmic order and are designed for meditation. Indeed, he says, the Flower itself is a mandala-symbol: it can be imagined and depicted as a blossom springing from a plant which is frequently 'a structure of brilliant fiery colours growing out of a bed of darkness, and carrying the blossom of light at the top'. In some mandalas, he adds, growth is the result of 'fire penetrating the seed'. Tippett in his autobiography writes that 'the wonderful mandalas in *The Secret of the Golden Flower* became embedded in my mind'; it's no surprise then that they bore fruit in his opera. So in the final version of its climax, King Fisher's stripping of Sosostris's veils reveals a dim glow which soon becomes 'an incandescent bud'. The bud begins to open and, once it is 'fully open like huge lotus petals on the stage [forming] a circle on the ground', the lovers are revealed in 'radiant transfiguration', the power of which fells King Fisher.[177] After the King's obsequies, the dancers 'appear by incantatory gestures to cause the lotus petals or other veils to close themselves back' over the lovers, at which 'the veiled mass glows from within and breaks into flame.' The 'precious pair of golden fishes' framed by the net in *Aurora Consurgens* become the lovers in the lotus; the net's ability to entangle the king becomes the power of the revealed pair to quell him with a look; and 'the Word, the great net circling heaven and earth,' becomes a lotus-mandala circling the stage.

177 Flower appears: *Secret*, 60, 69. Wilhelm's diagram: *Secret*, 74. Mandalas: *Secret*, 98 (cf. Jung, *Integration of the Personality*, 127: 'Eastern mandalas [...] are even represented bodily in certain ritualistic celebrations'). Mandalas embedded: *C20 Blues*, 89. Cf. A. Whittall, *The Music of Britten and Tippett* (Cambridge, 1982), 136.

Image 7.2 Mandala from Richard Wilhelm, *The Secret of the Golden Flower* (1931).

For such informed Taoists as can pick it up, there is a strong sense of Wilhelm and Jung moving behind the scenes here; but at the same time the lotus is such a universally apprehended symbol of fecundity and renewal that recognising the Taoist strain isn't essential to an audience's response, any more than is another allusive strain permeating this scene that resonates for those who are attuned to it: one that, although present in the February 1944 scenario (where 'G and M appear in the attitudes of an Eastern god and his mate'), is not firmed up till quite late on in the making of the final text. This is the Hindu image of the lotus as the throne of Shiva, with the god embracing his bride-emanation, Shakti/Parvati.[178] More 'primitively', the lotus circle also

178 In this connection, see n. 188 below for MT's gratitude for and acknowledgement of H. Zimmer's *Myths and Symbols in Indian Art and Civilization,* ed. J. Campbell (Washington DC, 1946), where the crucial Shiva-Shakti pages are pp. 137–48, with Fig. 34. But as early as 1940 he had almost certainly read some lines in Jung's *Integration of the Personality* about Shiva-Shakti mandalas that may well lie behind his 1944 reference to 'an Eastern god and his mate': 'The mandalas employed in [Indian] ceremonial always have great importance, for they contain at the centre a figure of the highest religious significance', for instance 'Shiva himself — generally embracing the Shakti' (*Integration*, p. 128). In European parallel, the revelation of Mark and Jenifer enthroned is perhaps also a conscious

connects with the circle of singers, pipers and drummers of the ancient Black Sea coast who surround the booth-platform on which the Marob King and Queen perform their Ploughing Eve mating dance in Naomi Mitchison's *The Corn King and the Spring Queen*, a novel of the early 1930s acknowledged by Tippett as 'a big influence' on this scene; present too are those pan-European midsummer fire-festivals described eloquently in earlier parts of that 'Balder' chapter of Frazer's and evoked in the first movement of Eliot's second Quartet, 'East Coker': festivals with their Christian links to the Feast of St John the Baptist ('Fire! Fire! St John's Fire...') and their pagan promise of fecundity to man and beast if they make contact with the flames.[179]

Ancient religious systems are present, then, but they don't insist on being consciously identified. On a multi-faith plane Tippett is doing what the newly converted T. S. Eliot in 1928 described as being done within a purely Christian framework by one Charles Claye in his *Merry Masque of Our Lady of London Town*. Noting that 'for the spoken scenes of the Masque the author has drawn on the liturgy and on old carols' and giving several examples of the procedure, Eliot insists that 'to make these observations is not to imply that the Masque is merely a tissue of allusions intelligible only to liturgical scholars [...]. The Masque that Mr Claye has written should appeal to everyone according to his knowledge.'[180] To which, *re* his own work, Tippett might want to add 'according to the access he has to the archetypes of the collective unconscious'; for here at the opera's climax he is surely reaffirming things he had said in the earlier 1940s to Newton, Allinson, Ayerst and Glock about his intentions for the piece: to make something 'contemporary or artistic/symbolic' out of the 'conjunction and

---

echo of the seventeenth-century Stuart court masque, especially of a particular epiphany-device of Ben Jonson's, to be seen for instance at the moment in his *Time Vindicated* when to 'loud music [...] the whole scene opens, where Saturn sitting with Venus is discovered above'.

179 *The Corn King and the Spring Queen* (London, 1931), III.ii; see *C20 Blues*, 259. (A draft late in 1949 for the chorus's text in the finale—Second Sketchbook, Add. MS 72055, 70r—refers to the lovers as 'corn-king and spring queen [...] the royal pair'.) MT could have found a precedent for putting such fire-ceremonies on stage in Roberto Gerhard's never fully realised ballet-project of the 1930s, *Soirées de Barcelone*, the original title of which had been *Les feux de Saint Jean*. This was to present rites and festivities of love and marriage at Midsummer in a Catalan village square and an enchanted forest nearby. (Gerhard like Newton was a Cambridge resident in the 1940s; one could speculate about a meeting.) For *Soirées*, see D. Drew in *Tempo*, 139 (1981), 20–21.

180 Eliot's note on *The Merry Masque* (1928), reprinted in the pamphlet by S. Revell, '*Not in Gallup*' (Oxford, 1988).

deposit of all sorts of ideas and interests'; to be 'syncretistic of course' in fashioning 'a symbol [...] which cannot be plucked to pieces either intellectually or from sensibility', and to 'incorporate and refashion [a] chorus of traditions' in a way that will work on a modern audience suggestively, since 'one can't manufacture a speculum for the deep things except out of indefiniteness.'[181] As he would put it to Barbara Hepworth about ten years later:

> The whole thing is this curious play between our sense in the theatre (what we hear and see) and shall we say, the collective unconscious, that given the symbol (not the fact) rises up to greet the image; and the timeless moment is created.

Although the mood of the veils-and-petals scene is very different from that of the purgatorial final paragraph of *The Waste Land*, Tippett's technique of multiple allusion is related to Eliot's own; so it is no surprise that at the very end of one draft of the opera's finale, after the incorporation of lines from Yeats's 'Lapis Lazuli' that survive into the final text ('All things fall and are built again...'), Tippett should write the last word of *The Waste Land*, 'Shantih', followed by an exclamation-point and a question-mark. It isn't clear, though, whether the quotation is a private sigh of relief on Tippett's part at a task completed or a passing notion that the word might possibly be sung as a kind of Amen Chorus at the end of the opera.[182]

The bearer of the fire to the lovers and their lotus is Strephon, and his role in this also grows out of ideas current in the *Aurora* years and before. According to the stage-direction in the published libretto, Strephon makes fire in the ancient friction-of-wood-drawn-through-wood way, recalling both Frazer's fire-chapter (which explains how that was done) and Jung's argument in *Psychology of the Unconscious* that this woodcraft-method was archetypally coital, so making it apt to a fire-making that will set the great love-lotus alight.[183]

181 Edward Dent, who admired *Midsummer Marriage*, observed to MT that 'the obscurity of your opera is due to the mix-up of several different symbolisms, though you may maintain that they are all the same in ultimate reality': quoted in Bowen, *Michael Tippett*, 34.

182 'The whole thing...': Schuttenhelm, *Selected Letters*, 356. 'Shantih!?': Add. MS 72055, 71r. Writing to George Barnes, director of the BBC Third Programme, on July 13 1947, MT describes his opera as 'a sort of Magic Flute story that will please Tom Eliot, yourself, I should say, and few else. But it seems it's got to come.' (Quoted by H. Carpenter, *The Envy of the World* [London, 1996], 63.)

183 Jung, *Psychology of the Unconscious*, tr. B. Hinkle (London, 1919), 87–105.

The stage-direction also requires that Strephon be assisted in the making by another dancer (female most like) who holds the block while he twirls the stick. She is one further emanation, surely, of Strephon's Girl, the mysterious creature who had danced the 'Windrose' with him in the 1944 scenario. In the completed opera she could be said to become a fourfold figure, her other three emanations being the Hound, Otter and Hawk who hunt Strephon's Hare, Fish and Small Bird more and more menacingly in the Ritual Dances of Act II. All three pursuing creatures were danced by the one dancer, Julia Farron, at the opera's 1955 premiere, with which Tippett was closely involved: an indication perhaps that the Strephon-Girl plot in its earlier form still had a shadowy presence in the finished opera.[184] Although, in line with Tippett's view in 1944, the Girl is not given a name in the *dramatis personae*, she is certainly a consequential figure. Her being nameless and her manifesting herself in four incarnations suggest that she is primarily there to embody the fruits of Strephon's imagination; but it is through her presence that the work's eightsome aspect is maintained.[185] The diagonal of Imaginative Boy and Imaginative or perhaps Imagined Girl keeps its place in the *I Ching*-related octagon (albeit an octagon that has now mutated into a decagon through the increasingly active involvement of the two Ancients).

This maintaining of links between collaboration-time in the early 1940s and *solus*-time in the late can be found in other parts of the piece too. For instance, when the plot still centred on the barrel, fish and net, Tippett had an idea that 'Sosostris, when she comes to her part, lays it on pretty thick, in the "O Isis and Osiris" style before she delivers the oracle.'[186] It was a concept which, however much has changed around the lady in plot terms, is carried through into the *Marriage* in its final form with the formidable aria 'Who hopes to conjure with the world of dreams'. Again, though the eating, drinking and partying of the chorus at curtain-up on the opera's last act don't appear in the 1944 scenario (since the occasion for them only arose when Tippett

184 In MT's sketch for the 'Race Dances' in the Second Sketchbook, Add. MS 72055, 45v-46v, the pursuing creatures are all danced by the same girl. (Strephon's fire-making assistant is definitely female in the draft in the Sixth Sketchbook, Add. MS 72059, 31r.)

185 Her presence seems to have made the Faun of earlier draft-scenes redundant; he certainly disappears from the plot. MT may also have come to consider him Old Hat. After all, it was fully 30 years since Max Beerbohm—paragraph 6 of 'Hilary Maltby and Stephen Braxton' (1917) in *Seven Men* (London, 1919)—had declared the pre-Great War vogue for fauns in the arts *over*.

186 BL292.93–4 (?March 1945). 'O Isis and Osiris': Sarastro in *The Magic Flute* II.i.

divided the original Act II into two separate acts in 1946 and found himself needing a striking opening scene for the second of them), evidence from the early 1940s and before suggests how natural it would have been to bring on party-goers and provide a particular menu for them. Cornford, scrutinised by composer and librettist in 1943–44, had maintained that a feast was integral to Aristophanic comedy, and Weston was on hand to suggest the form it should take, assuming King Fisher (who has summoned the chorus to the event) is footing the bill for it. It has to be a loaves, wine and fishes picnic, for this menu, she said, linked the Fisher King's cuisine back to ancient Jewish practice and that of the early Christian church: 'The Catacombs supply us with numerous illustrations [...]. The elements of this mystic meal were Fish, Bread, and Wine.'[187]

187 *From Ritual to Romance*, 129.

8 Echoes and foreshadowings

The feast that opens the newly shaped Act III is only one instance of what one can argue much more broadly: that the composer's reading in the 1930s and the War years gave him most of the basic materials that he needed (beyond his own imaginings) for the libretto of *Midsummer Marriage*, not only in its *Aurora Consurgens* form but in its final one. True, as several observers have pointed out, he did look carefully at new books in the later 1940s, three particularly: the *Myths and Symbols in Indian Art and Civilization* (1946) of Jung's admired friend Heinrich Zimmer, and two that came out in 1948: Robert Graves's *White Goddess: A Historical Grammar of Poetic Myth* and Gertrude Levy's *The Gate of Horn: A Study of the Religious Conceptions of the Stone Age, and Their Influence upon European Thought.*

He told his friend Anna Kallin in 1952 that Zimmer's book 'provided the last flower' in the *Marriage*'s tree-like growth; it clearly contributed to the Shiva-Shakti strand in the polyphony of symbols and traditions around the appearance of the transfigured Mark and Jenifer in Act III. The 'White Goddess' concept quite quickly entered Tippett's vocabulary in letters and was in time associated with the rising moon in the opera's third-act feast-chorus, while *The Gate of Horn*, Tippett told David Ayerst in 1948, was 'very good', 'most absorbing', and helped him 'no end to deepen the opera and traditionalise the imagery'.[188] Yet it's very likely that the actual inspirations for the opera's

188 Kallin/Zimmer: Schuttenhelm, *Selected Letters*, 363. *White Goddess*: see n. 198 below. MT to Ayerst *re* Levy: Schuttenhelm, *Selected Letters*, 244 (cf. *Selected Letters*, 363: MT to Kallin). *Re* Zimmer, see Kemp, *Tippett*, 491–2 (= n. 81). MT may well have known an earlier book of Zimmer's on Indian art, his *Kunstform und Yoga*, since it was recommended by Jung in 1940 in *The Integration of the Personality*, 127. Phrases from *Kunstform* (pp. 214 and 30 in the much later English translation: *Artistic Form and Yoga in the Sacred Images of India*, tr. G. Chapple

developing scenario ran all the deeper for being some years older than any of these books. Certainly the genesis of two important episodes suggests this.

Take the episode of Mark and Jenifer's big arias late in Act I — Mark's first of all. It may well be that Levy's vivid evocations of experiences below ground, extreme caving especially, helped nourish Tippett's imagination as he was composing Mark's monologue of his subterranean visit in its final form.[189] But, as we have seen, our collaborators had declared their source for Mark's 'drowned-world' journey in their draft Foreword to the *Aurora Consurgens* libretto three or four years before Levy's book appeared, and had declared it in a way that suggested significant ancillary sources in books of the 1930s and early 1940s. Says that Foreword: 'the Drowned World is of course the res - mersas of Vergil' — which is an assertion with two intriguing oddities. First, 'drowned world' is a pretty free translation of the 'res alta terra et caligine mersas' in the account of Aeneas' setting out in search of his dead father in Virgil's *Aeneid* Book VI, but is the translation Maud Bodkin had offered when discussing the scene in an essay on heaven-hell symbolism in her Jungian *Archetypal Patterns in Poetry: Psychological Studies of Imagination* in 1934: a book Tippett knew, [190] was fond of and is surely recalling here. Second, the spelling Vergil-with-an-'e' was rare in Britain before the 1950s but was characteristic of W. Jackson Knight in his singular *Cumaean Gates* and *Roman Vergil*. Tippett asked Newton to find him a copy of *Roman Vergil* when it came out from Faber's in 1944. (The Virgil-loving T. S. Eliot had been happy for his firm to publish it.) The earlier *Cumaean Gates* was an archaeological-anthropological, Jung-Eliot-and-Bodkin-quoting grand tour of the ancient Mediterranean and timeless Pacific, inspired by the account in *Aeneid* VI of the carving of a labyrinth in a temple near the Sibyl's Cumaean cave seen by Aeneas before he goes on his journey underground. Did Tippett know it? It is likely, not only because Knight's enthusiasm for Jung, Eliot and Bodkin would have

---

and J. Lawson [Princeton, 1984]) are close to the 'St John's Fire' chorus beginning 'Carnal love through which the race...' and to Mark's morning greeting ('After the visionary night...') in Act III of the opera's final text.

189 G. Levy, *The Gate of Horn* (London, 1948), 11–3. For further instances of Levy's presence in the libretto (and other germane matters besides), see R. Elfyn Jones, 'Ritual, Myth and Drama', in G. Lewis, ed., *Michael Tippett O.M.: A Celebration* (Tunbridge Wells, 1985), 59–72.

190 See Schuttenhelm, *Selected Letters*, 244, where MT describes Levy's new book as plucking 'the chords of our race-old memories, in the proper Bodkin: *Archetypal Patterns in Poetry* manner'.

appealed, but because the book acknowledges a debt to the fieldwork carried out among the 'Stone Men' of the Melanesian South Sea Islands by the anthropologist-psychologist John Layard. Layard and Knight were friends who appreciated each other's research, and for a period in the early 1940s Layard acted as Jungian analyst to the psychologically troubled Knight.[191] A couple of years before, Layard had been Tippett's analyst and had become his friend too: a friendship which lasted well into the 1940s. This suggests interactions. Mark's journey from the hilltop cave to the Dionysian Fields in *The Midsummer Marriage* certainly makes increased sense if read as reflecting lines from Virgil as they were expounded, expanded and troped by Bodkin and Knight.

Mark evokes the journey in dialogue with the Chorus:

> When I passed the gate of horn,
> What happened then, reading the riddle right? [...]
> Down, downwards to the centre.
> Doubled downwards,
> Crawling, falling,
> Rocked in a boat across the water
> Coldly lapping
> The waste land
> To thread the labyrinthine maze
> Of fear that guards the lovely meadows.

Put that beside Bodkin pondering Aeneas's underworld journey and other ancient ordeals of initiation:

> At the first entering of the cavern we are confronted with the horror of stench, darkness, yawning void; but as the journey proceeds, [...] the 'drowned world' appears as one of spiritual torment, [that of a man] plunging into the depths of his own being. [...] Virgil's phrase of the drowned world, *res . . . mersas,* has its parallel [in Dante's *Inferno*]: 'Let us descend into the blind world here below.' [...] [As Plutarch says of analogous initiation-rites:] There are wanderings and laborious circuits and journeyings through the dark, full of misgivings [...]; then before the end, come terrors of every

191 Copy of *Roman Vergil*: BL292.134 (19 Sept 1945). For Layard generally, see Chapter 2 of J. MacClancy, *Anthropology in the Public Arena* (Chichester, 2013). For Knight and Layard: see G. Wilson Knight, *Jackson Knight: A Biography* (Oxford, 1975), 163, 242–7, 268.

> kind [...]. After this a wonderful light meets the wanderer; he is admitted into pure meadowlands, where are voices and dances.

Plunging into the depths, achieving the meadowlands... And the boat, the Waste Land littoral and the guardian-labyrinth of Mark's aria? They are in Knight's *Cumaean Gates*. The use of labyrinths and mazes as place-protectors is one of the book's major themes, and Knight's excursion at one point into the land of the Grail Romances includes a glimpse of the coast later seen by Mark:

> The [Grail legend's] root ideas [...] centre on a mysterious Castle or Temple, situated always by water [...]. The country round the Castle is the Waste Land [...]. The difficulties in the way of finding the Grail Temple are both numerous and fearsome. [...] In several versions, however, the Quester is met by a boatman who [...] rows him across to the Island Temple.

Knight explicitly connects this boatman with Charon, ferryman of the underworld in Virgil, and he sets up a further parallel voyage: the Melanesian narrative he derives from Layard of the new ghosts of recently deceased South Sea Islanders progressing from a cave sometimes fronted by a labyrinth to the waterside and then by ferry to the island of the dead.[192] So although Tippett wrote to Ayerst that Gertrude Levy's work (which several times acknowledges the work of Knight, Bodkin and Layard) was helpful to him, 'particularly for the "hell" aria', it seems more likely that it was those 1930s books that give him the wherewithal, almost wholly in passages are not cited or quoted by Levy.[193]

Something similar seems to apply to Jenifer's corresponding 'heaven' aria:

> Then the congregation of the stars began
> To dance: while I in pure delight
> Saw how my soul flowered at the sight

192 Bodkin, *Archetypal Patterns in Poetry* (London, 1934), 127, 125. Knight, *Cumaean Gates* (Oxford, 1936), 143–5, 147, 13–8. *Re* Layard's journeying ghosts: even aside from very likely face-to-face discussions with him on the topic, MT could have encountered printed accounts of the Melanesian narrative in Layard's essay 'Der Mythos der Totenfahrt auf Melanesia', *Eranos Jahrbuch 1937* (Zürich, 1938), 241–91, and in his *Stone Men of Malekula*, 225–31, 649–55, etc.

193 Levy does refer to the passage from Plutarch that Bodkin had quoted: *Gate of Horn*, 297.

And leaving the body forward ran
To dance as well.

The ideas behind this, the musical treatment and perhaps the words too had been determined by 1944–45. The draft libretto's Foreword of those years tells us that the concept of the 'Heavenly Dance' evoked in Jenifer's aria came from *Orchestra: or A Poem of Dancing* by the Elizabethan Sir John Davies: a poem which sees dancing as informing and animating the whole cosmos. Davies's heroine Penelope foreshadows Jenifer:

What eye doth see the heaven, but doth admire
When it the movings of the heavens doth see?
Myself, if I to heaven may once aspire,
If that be dancing, will a dancer be.[194]

Writing to Newton in 1945 about the possibility of putting such celestial dancing physically into the action of *Aurora*, Tippett suggests that 'the way there may be via the Elizabethan World Picture', the capital letters making it clear that the collaborators had to hand the book of that name by Eustace Tillyard published in 1943, the closing chapters of which focus on *Orchestra*. But behind all this is Maud Bodkin again and her essay on 'The Archetype of Paradise - Hades' in *Archetypal Patterns*. There she writes of the opening of the Thirteenth Canto of Dante's *Paradiso*:

> When he would convey some image [...] of the dance that circled round him in the fourth heaven, Dante prays the reader to hold like a rock an image of the circling of the brightest stars visible in sundry regions of the sky [...], [for] the vast circling of the planets and of the starry heavens [...] can [...] be realized with imaginative sympathy, as constituting a cosmic dance in which the spirit of man may participate.[195]

194 Davies, *Orchestra*, stanza 26: E. Jones, ed., *The New Oxford Book of Sixteenth Century Verse* (Oxford, 1991), 656.

195 Tillyard: BL292.94 (March 1945). Bodkin: *Archetypal Patterns,* 145–6. (MT's notion of the cosmic dance links with his fish-and-net symbolisms. In a letter to Newton of spring 1945—BL292.94—he declares that 'the net and fishes is a symbol of heaven descending to hell: the net is a yang symbol and the fish a yin. Perhaps Margaret [= Jenifer] comes near a paradigm of the net operation, the net dance, or whatever, in heaven.')

The other important episode with strong echoes of the late 1930s and early 1940s is the sequence of Ritual Dances that put the spotlight on Strephon and the Neophyte troupe. In choosing animals in conflict as their dominant metaphor, Tippett could well have been building on an element of the phantom choral work he dreamed of in February 1939 since, as well as featuring fishing and a magic net, it had also developed an 'antithetic pair of metaphors' in the form of 'two antithetic animal symbols'. Most likely devising the dances as a coherent quartet in 1946–48, Tippett at first planned to place all four at the beginning of the new interlude-like Second Act that the opera had 'grown' (an enlargement of the beginning of its old Act II) — to put them, that's to say, in the place set aside in the surviving 1944 scenario for the 'Windrose' episode of Strephon and his Girl. They would have been followed by that newly devised marriage-proposal scene for Bella and Jack, with Bella taking the initiative. However, as we have seen, in September 1949, near the start of intensive composition-work on the act, there were some second thoughts, with the group of dances being moved to the *middle* of the new act and the last dance hived off and given a modified subject and new niche in the climactic scene of Act III. So now there was a sequence of three dance-rituals embedded in Act II: pursuit-dances for 'antithetic animals', erotic on one level, since the pursuer in each case is female and the pursued male (so connecting Darwinianly-Shavianly with Bella and Jack), and on another level so-to-speak heraldic—*à la* Lion and Unicorn—since the paired animals are of different species or genera. (It has been argued that on this level they connect with the world-views of Jenifer and Mark: *anima* becoming ever more concerned to bring *animus* to heel.)[196]

The inspiration for the new dance sequence has sometimes been traced to Graves's *White Goddess* of 1948.[197] As we've seen, it's a book that Tippett knew, and it certainly makes great play with the mythical episode from which the composer took situations for his dances: an episode to be found in the sixteenth-century Welsh 'Hanes Taliesin'

196 'Antithetic pair of metaphors': *C20 Blues*, 85. (See Second Sketchbook in Appendix III below for a *circa* 1946–48 draft scenario of the dance-scene followed by Bella and Jack's entrance.) *Anima-animus*: A cogent case is made by J. Lloyd Davies, p. 58 of "A Visionary Night", in N. John, ed., *The Operas of Michael Tippett* (London, 1985), 53–62. Cf. Kemp, *Tippett,* 221–2.

197 Kemp argues the case that the Graves was the prime influence in *Tippett*, 230–31, as does R. Elfyn Jones, pp. 65–6 of 'Myth, Ritual and Drama' in Lewis, ed., *Michael Tippett O.M.*; cf. Jones's *Early Operas of Michael Tippett* (Lewiston, 1996), 42–3 etc. J. Lloyd Davies concurs: "A Visionary Night", in John, ed., *Operas of Michael Tippett*, 58.

narrative which Charlotte Guest had made part of the *Mabinogion* she assembled in 1838–49 (though more recent scholars concur that it doesn't really belong there). The 'Hanes Taliesin' presents the cunning-woman Ceridwen and her laboratory-assistant Gwion as hunter and quarry four times over in four bursts of animal-disguise. Writing to White, Tippett once went so far as to describe his dances in Graves's language as 'ritualistic leading if permitted to the death and dismemberment of the Year King in the Service of the White Goddess'.[198] But again the roots stretch further back. As early as 1939, in the midst of the curative phase of Jungian dream-analysis that was set going for him by John Layard (one of its dreams featuring that art-work based on 'antithetic animal symbols'), Tippett was reading *Problems of Mysticism and Its Symbolism* by an associate of Jung's, Herbert Silberer, and that book too alludes to Guest's re-telling of the Ceridwen-Gwion episode in the 'Tale of Taliesin' — indeed, it quotes from it *in extenso* during a discussion of Introversion and Regeneration. As the English translation of the Silberer that Tippett knew has it, Gwion, fleeing the furious Ceridwen but accidentally gifted with shape-shifting powers, saw her

> from a distance and turned into a hare and redoubled his speed, but she at once became a hound, forced him to turn around and chased him towards a river. He jumped in and became a fish, but his enemy pursued him quickly in the shape of an otter, so that he had to assume the form of a bird and fly up into the air. But the element gave him no place of refuge, for the woman became a falcon, came after him and would have caught him [...]. Trembling for fear of death he saw a heap of smooth wheat on a threshing floor, fell into the middle of it, and turned into a grain of wheat. But Ceridwen took the shape of a black hen, flew to the wheat, scratched it asunder, recognized the grain and swallowed it [thereby conceiving the bard Taliesin].[199]

198 Graves's *Mabinogion* citings: *The White Goddess* (London, 1948), 24, 352–3, etc. *White Goddess* in MT letters: White, *Tippett*, 54, 59. (Douglas Newton too knew *The White Goddess* and seems to have admired it; in a review of Auden's *Enchafèd Flood* he describes the Graves as likely to father 'an exceedingly numerous and healthy family': *Poetry London*, 6 [Winter, 1951], 30.) MT to White on the dances: White, *Tippett*, 53–4. (White there has '[Sear?] King', but a Frazerian 'Year King' is more likely.)

199 MT reading Silberer in English: *C20 Blues*, 92–3. Transcribing from Guest's *Mabinogion*: Silberer, *Problems of Mysticism and Its Symbolism*, tr. S. Jelliffe (New York, 1917), 310–11. Silberer had found Guest's narrative in German translation

In Guest/Silberer's narrative, these animal pairings come only a few sentences after Gwion's being imbued by drops from Ceridwen's magic cauldron with knowledge of 'everything that was to come'. In his barrel-net-fish phase, Tippett had perhaps read onwards from the cauldron episode and been struck by the idea that he might one day make a chain of dances relating to the chase episode. 'Racing dances' was his first name for them when he actually did so: Hound *vs* Hare, Otter *vs* Fish, Hawk *vs* Small Bird, Hen *vs* Grain of Wheat. He could have been encouraged in such ritual race-making by memories of the admired *Themis* of Jane Harrison and friends ('a decisive book', he called it), which has a chapter on 'The Origin of the Olympic Games' contributed by Francis Cornford that pinpoints a particularly interesting ritual race run at the Karneian Games in ancient Laconia: one that took an 'older form' than mere competitive athletics. In it,

> the young man, decked with garlands and perhaps also disguised with the skin of a beast so as to be the 'mumming representative of a *daimon*', embodies the luck of the year, which will be captured or lost, according as the youth is overtaken or escapes.

There may have been encouragement too in Maud Bodkin's concurring with Harrison in regarding 'the ritual dance, and other such ceremonies, as imaginative achievements having potential social value through influence over group-attitudes toward the unknown forces of reality'.[200] Tippett arranged that his dances should have a powerful effect on one character at least: the impressionable Bella. In an earlier phase of drafting, Bella had found it vexing enough to stumble on Strephon with Parthenia and the Faun. Now, in the final version of the text, her seeing and interrupting the climax of the Hawk-Bird dance as the Hawk comes close to killing the Bird touches her at an even deeper level. (Her response again is 'I wasn't born for all these mysteries.')

---

in F. Nork's *Mythologie der Volkssagen und Volksmärchen* of the 1840s. (*Problems of Mysticism* was re-issued in 1971 as *The Hidden Symbolism of Alchemy and the Occult Arts*. It was a book Jung had considered 'admirable' and 'very able': Jung, *Two Essays on Analytical Psychology*, tr. H. and C. Baynes [London, 1928], 85 and 243.)

200 'Racing dances': White, *Tippett*, 53. 'Decisive book': MT to Anna Kallin in Schuttenhelm, *Selected Letters*, 363. Harrison (with Murray and Cornford), *Themis: A Study in the Social Origin of Greek Religion* (Cambridge, 1912), 234. Bodkin: *Archetypal Patterns*, 331. Around 1939 (*C20 Blues*, 89), Arthur Waley's partner Beryl de Zoete had given MT a copy of her *Dance and Drama in Bali* (London, 1938), which evokes—pp. 25–6, 46, 52–3, 57, etc.—animal dances, temple dances, libation dances and ritual dances.

The chain of dances she disturbs is a nice instance of Tippett's 'manufacturing a speculum for the deep things'. Speculatively, one can imagine him taking his Pursuers and Pursued (four pairs initially) from Silberer's *Problems*, coming on Graves's assertion in *The White Goddess* that the four chases were in seasonal sequence (hare in autumn, fish in winter, bird in spring, grain in summer), and then recalling that each of the seasons evoked in T. S. Eliot's recent *Four Quartets*—one per Quartet—was linked with a particular element (spring with air, summer with earth, autumn with water, winter with fire). He duly borrows Eliot's idea, though he puts the elements in a different order relative to the seasons (hare-autumn-earth, fish-winter-water, bird-spring-air, grain-summer-fire). In early September 1949, as White tells us, he transforms the quarry of the fourth dance from a speck of grain to a full-grown human being—seed into the bearer of seed—and transfers the dance itself to Act III. Then a few days later, he happens on the young Norman Jeffares's recent study, *W. B. Yeats: Man and Poet*, where he is struck by the evidence in it from the poet's letters that, in Yeats's pithy Blakean poem 'The Four Ages' (from the 'Supernatural Songs' of 1935), each of the elements corresponds cryptically to one of the Ages of Man. Yeats's 'fascinating allied stuff' intrigues Tippett.[201] A grid seems to be forming:

[Silberer/MT]		*[RG]*		*[TSE]*		*[WBY]*
flesh	—	autumn	—	earth	—	childhood, body, instinct
fish	—	winter	—	water	—	youth, heart, passion
fowl	—	spring	—	air	—	maturity, mind, thought
grain/man	—	summer	—	fire	—	mortality, the soul, God

On one level the grid recalls the kinds of categories that had attached themselves to the trigrams of the *I Ching* in ancient China. On another it dictates that the four dances shall peak in a fire-dance involving a ritual human death.

201 Graves's seasons: *White Goddess*, 352–3. Eliot's elements: In the 1940s the poet himself was telling interested readers about the *Quartets*' season-element links (Ricks and McCue, *Poems of T. S. Eliot*, 1.900). Events in Sept 1949 and Yeats' 'Four Ages': White, *Tippett*, 52–8, and A. Jeffares, *W. B. Yeats: Man and Poet* (London, 1949), 283–4. The Yeats letters that Jeffares calls on are to be found in A. Wade, ed., *The Letters of W. B. Yeats* (London, 1954), 823–6. In the original *Hanes Taliesin*, the transformations seem to lack seasonal or elemental overtones; see J. Wood, 'The Folklore Background of the Gwion Bach Section of *Hanes Taliesin*', *Bulletin of the Board of Celtic Studies*, 29 (1980–82), 621–34, pp. 629ff.

Image 8.1 Malekulan Hawk-Banners, 1915, drawing by John Layard from his *Stone Men of Malekula* (1942); *courtesy of the Estate of John Layard.*

The fire-dance itself would be held back until the opera's Act III, where Tippett's mandala ritual provided a context for it; but how were those pursued and pursuing beasts in Act II to be imagined as dancing? John Layard may have been helpful. His *Stone Men of Malekula*, the massive account of his fieldwork on the islands of Atchin and Vao in what was then the New Hebrides and is now Vanuatu, came out in 1942 (the year Tippett invited him to a dinner party after the première of the *Fantasia on a Theme of Handel*). Tippett knew the book, and it's hard to believe that he didn't find germane things in it: those subterranean journeys of new ghosts, as we have seen — and perhaps the Atchin Islanders' cult of the hawk. Layard describes and illustrates the carved hawks that were perched on rooftrees and the giant hawk-kites that appeared at their 'Maki' festivals, and he evokes a ritual dance in which a formidable hawk made mayhem among lesser fowl:

> A yet more resplendent dancer [...] painted to represent a hawk and called 'the hawk pouncing on its prey' [...] dances round and in and out among ranks of Maki-men, at first in a peaceful

> way [...]. At a given moment, however, he adopts a threatening attitude. His body sways from side to side, his 'wings' raised first one side and then the other, till, finally, he [...] swoops down upon the mass of Maki-men representing small birds, who cower and shuffle, breaking formation to gather in a frightened formless mass around the feet of the 'hawk', who, with outstretched arms, stands in their midst surveying the carnage.[202]

If a pouncing Hawk could fly through 'the Air in Spring' in one Ritual Dance, a hunting Otter could swim through 'the Waters in Winter' in another. Jung himself had occasionally thought of otters as psychological symbols in the 1930s[203] and on a more mammalian level, Henry Williamson's *Tarka the Otter* had a big reputation at the time (and Tarka is a great fish-hunter). Tippett having dispensed with the *Mabinogion*'s Black Hen, that only left the Hare hunted by the Hound across 'the Earth in Autumn'. Enter Layard again, with his highly Jungian *Lady of the Hare*, which appeared in 1944, the year of the première of *A Child of Our Time*: a première Layard knew about and may well have attended. Tippett first saw *The Lady of the Hare* in draft form and, once published, gave it a special place on his shelf.[204] It sets very detailed analyses of a particular patient's dreams, one of them about the death of a hare, beside masses of hare lore from all over Europe, Asia, Africa and North America, much as Tippett the same year was counterpointing his phallic-fish dream with the quantity of evidence he found in Eisler about ancient pagan fish-cults. In the process, Layard quotes the poet W. R. Rodgers on hare-hunting in Northern Ireland:

> Any farmer's son who wants a hunt takes the horn and goes out and blows it, and immediately all the hounds within earshot come running. [...] The hare, they say, runs in a circle when hunted and

202 Handel dinner: *C20 Blues*, 134. Layard, *Stone Men of Malekula*, 338–9; cf. 273 (fig. 41), 373–5, 441 (fig. 53), 733–4. (Newton quotes a song-text from *Stone Men* in his essay of the mid-1940s, 'The Composer and the Music of Poetry'; see above, nn. 22 and 138.)

203 In *Integration of the Personality*, 73: an extension of the passage known to MT and quoted above, n. 85, about a proper searching of the psyche's depths; and in *The Symbolic Life (Collected Works,* Vol. 18: London, 1977), 762–4: an analysis of a children's story by Jung's friend Oskar Schmitz.

204 Oratorio première: announcement of it preserved in the Layard Papers, UC San Diego Library, Corresp. Box 16. MT's bookshelf and *The Lady of the Hare*: D. Ayerst in Kemp, ed., *Michael Tippett: A Symposium*, 67. (On *The Lady* and *Midsummer Marriage*, cf. R. Elfyn Jones, 'Music, Ritual and Drama', 66ff.)

> will come back to the place she started from. [...] She must be followed by scent.

— on which Layard observes:

> All spiritual knowledge 'goes in circles', that is to say it has to do with rebirth, which is itself a return to the beginning on a different psychological level, as opposed once more to logical deduction, which works in a straight line.[205]

Tippett seems to echo this in his stage-directions. To orchestral horn-calls, his hound 'begins to hunt the hare by scent', gets 'warmer on the scent' and finally 'gets the full scent', and the course designated for the chase contrasts with those for the other dances in being circular.[206]

Layard is at his most interesting and persuasive in his treatment of the 'sacrifice' of a hare—it was the crucial episode in the Lady of the Hare's dreams—and in his putting this into the context of folk-beliefs about the hare's *self*-sacrificial nature. It's tempting to suggest that some of this spilled over into 'Fire in Summer', Tippett's final dance for Strephon at the climax of Act III of the *Marriage*. When he assembled a continuous sequence of the four dances for concert use in 1953, he entitled this one 'The Voluntary Human Sacrifice', two years later incorporating that title into the brief plot synopsis he wrote for the programme of the opera's premiere at Covent Garden. The title glances in passing at Cornford's view that an Aristophanic comedy could not have a happy outcome unless there had first been a sacrifice, and possibly has links too with Gertrude Levy's account in *The Gate of Horn* of sacrificial rites in ancient Ur of the Chaldees.[207] But more significantly it recalls one of Layard's conversations with his patient in *The Lady of the Hare*. They had been talking of her dream-hare's willingness to be sacrificed, reflecting on

> the look of extreme satisfaction and trust that had been in the hare's eyes as it looked back at her when she plunged the knife into its back. We then talked about the nature of sacrifice, that it must be willing, that it must be of something perfect or of the highest

205 *The Lady of the Hare*, 184.

206 Purely orchestrally too, a Layard-like non-'progressive' movement is suggested by the use of a recurrent ground bass for the dance.

207 'On certain occasions [the shrine at Ur] would have been the scene of human sacrifice, which [...] may have been considered as voluntary and reciprocal between votary and God.' Levy, *The Gate of Horn*, 105.

> value. [...] Beasts may be free to do what they like but they are not human. Man in a primitive state may have been free to do what he liked, but had no knowledge of God. Being civilised had its advantages, but it entailed the sacrifice of the exercise of untrammelled instinct. [...] By sacrifice we willingly give up part of our primitive natural satisfaction in return for all that is entailed by civilisation and the spiritual benefits that true civilisation confers.[208]

In the book as a whole the hare stands as symbol for this. Layard cites the view of one of Rodgers's farmer friends that 'the hare really enjoys being hunted' and asks: 'What better symbolic image could be found of the basic truth enshrined in all "willing sacrifice" that instinct *wants to be* transformed into spirit?' Another piece of hare lore derives, he notes, from the animal's characteristic of not running away when the scrub around it is being burned,

> but of clinging to the last moment to its hiding place until the flames close in on it, and then wildly rushing out with fur blazing so that it burns to death. This, doubtless, is the material or physical fact that gave rise to the notion of the hare as a willing victim leaping into the fire. The symbolic meaning is another matter.[209]

Tippett's Strephon in the last Ritual Dance is something of a Layardian hare in human form in that he voluntarily sacrifices himself by fire. The stage-directions tell us that he makes fire and 'dances with the lighted stick', a recollection perhaps of designs for dancers with flambeaux that Inigo Jones painted for seventeenth-century masques by Chapman and Campion and/or of the Malekulan fire-dancer Layard himself had seen in 1915 and later drawn from a photograph for his *Stone Men* of 1942. He then strikes a pose at the feet of the transfigured lovers which suggests a 'hieratic pedestal'; other dancers take the fire from him, and it is raised over the lotus which, closing round the three of them, finally bursts into flame. Strephon's is an immolation by fire like that of the hare in Layard's book: the hare who 'transforms instinct into spirit'. (In the book Layard several times associates the animal with the Introverted-Intuitive character-type. Tippett, as we have seen, saw himself as Introverted-Intuitive: a further reason to link his dances for Strephon with Layard on hares and hare lore.)[210]

208 *The Lady of the Hare*, 63–4.
209 *The Lady of the Hare*, 185 and 106.
210 Transformation of instinct: see Layard, *Lady of the Hare*, 23, 63, 89, 112. The hare and the Jungian type: *Lady of the Hare*, 110–15, 197 (cf. 113n: 'It is with this

Image 8.2 John Layard, Malekulan Fire-Dancer, drawing from his *Stone Men of Malekula* (1942); *courtesy of the Estate of John Layard.*

'The Voluntary Human Sacrifice' turns out to be something of a play on words. On the level of pure theatre Strephon, urged and encouraged by fellow dancers who 'force him back towards the transformation of Mark and Jenifer', wills himself to take his own life, or rather to simulate so doing as part of the ritual. His is a sacrifice in the manner of the harvest-ensuring human sacrifices described in Frazer's *Golden Bough*—see the 'Lityerses' chapter in *Spirits of the Corn*—except that in this instance the victim offers himself to the fire freely. But what is symbolised by that ritual act, a mixture of magic and make-believe, is 'voluntary human sacrifice' in a different sense: the

introverted intuition that the mythological images dealt with in this book are concerned'). MT and the type: see n. 49 above. Layard quotes a germane Buddhist scripture of the Buddha himself reborn as a hare during his Bodhisattva phase and sacrificing himself to provide a meal for a starving Brahman: 'Offering his whole body as a free gift, [he] leapt up, and, like a royal swan alighting on a lotus bed, threw himself in an ecstasy of joy into the burning fire.' *Lady of the Hare*, 109–10.

willing sacrifice of part of themselves by wise human beings in order that they may achieve a healing unity with God, or the world, or each other — in Mark and Jenifer's case a relationship that's to be crowned by marriage. As Layard puts it in 1944, the exercise of untrammelled instinct has to be sacrificed in some measure to achieve civilisation, and as Tippett himself implies in the same year apropos Goodman's *Don Juan*, closeness to pure instinct is desirable, but it must only be to the degree that it doesn't compromise 'our never to be disvalued but dangerous intellect': an intellect which at its best can allow us visions of 'what knits or knots us together as a fraternity'. Strephon, the instinctive-imaginative artist, endorses this notion—signs it, so to speak—by becoming the mutually sacrificing pair's 'hieratic pedestal' during the climactic 'new dance' which the Ancients had promised Mark near the beginning of the opera.

All this underlines the significance of Strephon's name, for he is an embodiment of that Hellenic spirit which meant so much to Tippett in the 1930s and 1940s, and which forms a recurrent theme of his letters to Newton in 1943–44: the spirit of Hölderlinian Greekness as the best synthesis the West could offer of intellect and instinct, mind and body, order and impulse, light and shadow, civility and passion. Perhaps it was a synthesis not wholly repeatable in the modern world (though we would certainly get closer to it if we could show our unregenerate King Fishers the door); but it was one worth aspiring to, contemplating and keeping as a touchstone, as the 'classical Greece' that had achieved it was 'the core and source of nearly the whole western world civilisation'.[211] Early in the drafting of *Aurora*, Mark-as-George was at one point to have kissed Strephon, which Tippett glossed, on one level, as 'the modern embraces the Greek'. At the climax of the *Marriage*, they are emblematically close again.

True, this was only one Greece that the modern imagination might feed on. There was another: a Greece characterised, Tippett thought, by a 'dark demonism' that is also an 'integral part' of the complete Greek experience, a Greece subject to what the 1944 scenario describes as the 'Dionysiac frenzy' which can break out 'as an orgy of blood in total war'. (The meadows Mark visits below ground show signs of this dark potential: 'the beat of life inflamed by death,' the 'full Communion [of] Man with Beast and All in One'.) Interestingly, Newton's 1940s poems suggest that, if anything, *his* Greek preoccupation was more slanted towards that demonic Greece, especially as

211 BL291.101 (22 May 1943): Sch 151.

manifested in the Trojan War: an image, surely, of the total war he was himself taking pains at the time *not* to be part of. In one poem or another, Newton presents 'Troy's great mound, where cities / Lay caked in tiers', Agamemnon masked, Agamemnon again as a ghost, Ajax arming and Ulysses scheming *en route* home to Ithaca. [212] (His one published volume of selected poems would appropriately be called *Metamorphoses of Violence*.)

It would not be until the later 1950s and his next opera, *King Priam,* that Tippett himself would come to inhabit that darker Greece; but the death-beat, the torn animals and trampled children we register glancingly in Mark's underworld aren't the only signs that he was creatively aware of the dark-Dionysiac in the 1940s. In 1943 he asked Newton if he could find him a Homer translation; could he 'try to lay hands for me on a Pope's Iliad? I want to read it very much'. And in 1944 he was thinking of Edmund Wilson's use in *The Wound and the Bow* of the ancient myth of the warrior Philoctetes, evoked in *Iliad* Book II. 'What a subject for an opera', he said. [213] It is as if, during the genesis years of *Midsummer Marriage*, he already had inklings of a tragic Homeric complement to its comedy, with the unending cycle of male vengeance on the plains and at the citadel of Troy furnishing the requisite orgy of blood. The *Aurora* project, he had told David Ayerst, would be 'syncretistic of course, but leaning more to Apollo than Dionysus'. (To underline the fact, its plot would run from one sunrise to the next.) A Homeric opera could lean darkly the other way.

This 1940s foreshadowing wasn't unique. Several ideas, procedures and plot-elements considered or mooted in connection with *Aurora* but only used *en passant* or not at all in the *Marriage* recur, suitably modified, in later works of Tippett's, and a sketch of some of them may indicate the fertility of the thought that went into planning the Masque. An instance on the narrative level is the role originally given the Ancients as the presenters of an instructive show for their eager Neophyte charges: charges who, as we've seen, greet them in one draft-text with

> Ancient masters of the ceremonies,
> What have you fresh for us to see today?

212 'Dark demonism': BL291.147 (21 Oct 1943): Sch 159. 'Dionysiac frenzy': see the 1944 scenario, Scs 1 and 5 above. 'Troy's great mound': 'Onionskin Man' (see Appendix II). Agamemnon's mask: 'A Death-Mask' (in Appendix I).

213 'Pope's Iliad': BL291.119 (27 Sept 1943). Philoctetes: *C20 Blues*, 168. D. Clarke traces Dionysiac and Nietzschian links between the *Marriage* and *King Priam* in Ch. 3 of *The Music and Thought of Michael Tippett* (Cambridge, 2001), 36–95.

Metatheatrical presenters of various kinds persist through the operas, right up to *New Year*. The Masque's masters of the ceremonies look forward to the trio of Nurse, Old Man and Young Guard in *King Priam*, to the god Hermes too: figures who are sometimes inside but as often outside an action which for them is a story that they already know. ('Thus shall a story begin…'; 'Thus we follow the story…'; 'We shall see from the story…'; 'The story soon will end…') On a psychological plane meanwhile, the bisexuality that Tippett introduces early on in connection with Strephon and George, expressed in the Graeco-modern kiss of those 'otherwise spliced males', recurs in *Priam* in the closeness of Achilles (husband and father) to Patroclus, whom in Tippett's words 'he passionately loved'.[214] And these elements—a narrative within a narrative, a versatile Eros—return in the very different world of *The Knot Garden*. There metatheatre reigns. The opera's modern-day master of ceremonies, the psychoanalyst Mangus, imbues the action with reminiscences of Shakespeare's *The Tempest* and in the last act mounts a big, hopefully therapeutic charade based on the play. (Shades not only of the Masque's Ancients but of Mme Sosostris's suggestion in *Aurora*'s 1944 scenario that acting out a 'mythological drama' might resolve King Fisher's problems.) And it's a charade that, among other things, partly resolves the bisexual complications the opera has presented in scenes involving the married businessman Faber, the conflicted writer Mel and the Introverted-Intuitive musician Dov.

Mangus's dismissal of the charade leads to the 'Yellow Sands' ensemble: a telling extension of the *parabasis* mode Tippett had experimented with in plans for the Masque, had then given to the She-Ancient at the death of King Fisher in the *Marriage* and later to the Trojan serving-women in *Priam*. In the *Knot Garden*'s *parabasis*, the cast share an image to express their sense of togetherness:

> We sense the magic net
> That holds us veined
> Each to each to all.

That too harks back to *Aurora*: to the net out of Goethe that Strephon draws magically from the barrel, a symbol of the force that 'knits and knots us together'. (Where better to do that after all than in a knot-garden?) Similarly with the strong visual image of renewal in the climactic hospital scene of *The Ice Break*. There the troubled central

214 Bowen, *Tippett on Music*, 216.

character Yuri, encased in plaster after being brought near to death in a race-riot, is figuratively reborn by being cut out of his shell by a Nurse and Doctor. It is a magical, momentous scene, but somewhere behind it are the irony and knowingness of the episode near the end of the Masque where, in a blending of folk-drama and childsplay, Jack and Bella as Doctor and Nurse resurrect the seemingly defunct King Fisher.

And there's the matter of that octagon of trigrams that Tippett copied out at the beginning of the First Sketchbook. The character-octagon in *Aurora*, which I've suggested connects with ancient China through Wilhelm and Jung, becomes a polygon in the *Marriage* as the Ancients, presenters in the Masque, join more fully in the action. But those trigrams also make their presences felt in *King Priam, The Knot Garden* and perhaps *The Ice Break. Priam* has eight principal characters, divided into four couples. *The Knot Garden* was conceived as an eight-character piece, though as it grew it shed one of its eight (an ascetic lady-doctor, presumably a partner for the Prospero-figure Mangus). And with *The Ice Break* it is tempting, if one is avid for eightsomes and mindful of Tippett's concern with symbols of healing, to spirit up a further octet by complementing the opera's obvious sextet of principals (mature married couple + younger coloured couple + younger white couple) with a pair of contrasting healers: Luke, the serious, practical, reliable life-saving doctor, and the psychedelic Astron, that good-hearted but evanescent Cheshire Cat of a pop-guru. ('Saviour?! [...] Me!! You must be joking.') Seven years after *The Ice Break* we are on firmer ground: the 64 hexagrams of the *Book of Changes* are unequivocally present in 'The Beleaguered Friends', a scene near the end of *The Mask of Time.* (Its working title had been *The Song of Changes.*) There the *I Ching*, consulted in a situation of stress and crisis, responds with a sign of hope and healing: Hexagram Forty, the Hexagram of Deliverance, in which, Richard Wilhelm explains, 'the movement goes out of the sphere of danger. The obstacle has been removed, the difficulties are being resolved.'[215]

215 Eight-character *Knot Garden*: see White, *Tippett*, 95–6 and 100, and Schuttenhelm, *Selected Letters*, 382. *Song of Changes*: Soden, *Michael Tippett*, 564. Hexagram of Deliverance: Bowen, *Tippett on Music*, 254. Wilhelm, *The I Ching*, 154.

9 Afterlives

Ideas aired in the years of Tippett and Newton's collaboration over *Aurora Consurgens* had an afterlife, then, in Tippett's work beyond *Midsummer Marriage*. Newton's own enthusiasms and preoccupations had an afterlife too. 1944 was almost certainly the year in which he first met Mary Lee Settle; two years later they were married. They had eventful times together and made some lively contacts.[216] On a trip to Paris in the autumn of 1949, for instance, they met John Cage and Merce Cunningham, who like them were staying in the Rue St Louis, Cage putting them in touch with the young Pierre Boulez who lived nearby. (A little over a year later, Cage's 'chance music' project would receive a boost when he was given a copy of the just-published English translation of the Wilhelm-Jung *I Ching*.) They lived in various parts of southern England, in the West Country, but mainly in London. Den found work as an editor, essayist and reviewer — also, it is said, as a scriptwriter and producer at the BBC. Mary Lee became a freelance journalist, working at the same time on bigger projects, including her first published novel, *The Love Eaters* (1954), which she dedicated to Den, as two years earlier he had dedicated *Metamorphoses of Violence* to her. The British Museum was one focus of their lives: Mary Lee busy in the Reading Room researching sources for the series of historical novels she would write on life in her home state of Virginia; Den haunting the Museum's galleries once more, the ethnological ones especially. He got to know some young sculptors fascinated and inspired by tribal sculpture, among them William Turnbull and Eduardo Paolozzi. (Paolozzi was with Den and Mary Lee in Paris when Cage enthused to them about Boulez.) Den would have warmed to Robert Melville's 1947 recommendation of Paolozzi as a sculptor 'whose work

216 Settle, *Learning to Fly*, 147–57, 162–4, 176–7, 192–206.

is more barbaric and at the same time more classical in its casual poise than anything the English School can show', and in 1950 he would go so far as to buy a couple of Paolozzis. He was also getting to meet several notable anthropologists living in London, not least Raymond Firth, who had researched in the Malay States, New Guinea, the Solomon Islands and Maori New Zealand. The great archipelago to the east of Malaysia was coming back into focus.[217]

Along with all this, Newton's work as a journalist and art-critic allowed him, as he later put it, 'to gain some knowledge of graphics and exhibition-installation'. He gained hands-on experience in connection with the patriotic show of a different sort of tribal art at the Whitechapel Gallery in autumn 1951: '*Black Eyes and Lemonade*: A Festival of Britain Exhibition of British Popular and Traditional Art [...] Organized by Barbara Jones and Tom Ingram, and Catalogued by Douglas Newton.' Both Newtons lent items for the show. Barbara Jones was a pioneer of interest in 'popular' and 'vernacular' work—*Unsophisticated Arts*, her influential book related to the exhibition, appeared in 1951—and Newton became creatively involved with her circle. Late in the decade he would publish a genial mini-history, *Clowns* (dedicated to Mary Lee's parents-in-law by her first marriage, the Weathersbees) with pictures by Jones, and an anthology of *Hymns as Poetry* made in collaboration with Tom Ingram and dedicated to Jones and to Mary Lee. The book had a joint Introduction that allowed Newton to return one more time to the relation of words and music. However, museology rather than music was again becoming the centre of his life: so much so that he seems to have wanted to make a new start with it, and in a new country. The opportunity came in 1956 when his friend Porter McCray suggested that his knowledge, enthusiasm, skills and curatorial interests might fit him for a job at a museum that was soon to open in New York. Mary Lee, for professional and emotional reasons of her own, wanted to relocate in America, and their being a married couple would allow her husband to enter the U.S.A., take up residence and gain work quite legally. So, America it was for both of them — though they divorced soon afterwards. The marriage had soured, and Mary Lee had lost her heart to an all-American gentleman whom she had known since adolescence and now had to be with.[218]

217 Melville: *Horizon* (Sept. 1947), 212–3, quoted in J. Collins, *Eduardo Paolozzi* (Farnham, 2014), 32. Newton buys: Collins, *Paolozzi*, 57. British Museum and Firth: Mattet, 'Entretien', 20.

218 McCray and divorce: Mattet, 'Entretien', 22; Settle, *Learning to Fly*, 204–5.

Newton, however, was not left stranded and directionless in the States. Rather, he remarried and launched on a 45-year career which would make him a celebrated and revered figure in the world of Oceanic Art.[219] From 1957 on, he rose through the ranks of the Nelson Rockefeller — René d'Harnoncourt — Robert Goldwater Museum of Primitive Art, from Assistant Curator to (in 1974) Director: managing, acquiring, organising, exhibiting at the Museum and elsewhere—when Tippett first visited New York in 1965, did he call on his old friend there?—and going off for five periods of collecting and fieldwork in the East Sepik region of Papua New Guinea. In the mid-1970s Nelson Rockefeller ('a mediocre politician' in Newton's view but 'a great connoisseur') arranged for the transfer of his Museum's collections to the Metropolitan Museum of Art, most spectacularly to the new wing opened in 1982 in memory of Rockefeller's son Michael, who had drowned while researching and acquiring in New Guinea. Newton moved with the collections, eventually becoming chairman of the Metropolitan's Department of the Arts of Africa, Oceania and the Americas. He retired at the age of 70 in 1990, was made Curator Emeritus and was still active in his eighth decade. When he died on 19 September 2001, the journal *Pacific Arts* declared that he was 'the ultimate connoisseur', one whose 'lifetime of looking at the art of many cultures created an encyclopedic knowledge that he generously shared with many people'. He was, the journal said, 'a great man, indeed'. From his *Art Styles of the Papuan Gulf* of 1961 onwards, he had written, collaborated on or edited over two dozen books, mainly on Pacific-Oceanic subjects, and had been copious with encyclopaedia entries, introductions, journal articles and catalogue texts.[220] The slow pen of the 1940s, finding its metier, had speeded up prodigiously.

However, he seems not to have become any more Jungian in the interim. Thus, in an essay 'The Flat, the Round, and Space' in his book with Hermione Waterfield of 1995, *Tribal Sculpture*, he writes:

219 For Newton's American career, see pp. 22–30 of Mattet, 'Entretien'; also pp. 32–7 of E. Kjellgren, 'Returning to the Source'; V.-L. Webb, 'Douglas Newton (1920–2001)', *Pacific Arts* (2001), 171–2, and H. Cotter, 'Douglas Newton, 80, Curator Emeritus at the Metropolitan', *New York Times*, 22 Sept 2001.

220 'A great man, indeed': Webb, 'Douglas Newton', 172. His later publications include *Seafarers of the Pacific* (NY, 1964); *Crocodile and Cassowary* (NY, 1975); *Islands and Ancestors: Indigenous Styles in South-east Asia* (Munich, 1989) with J. Barbier; *Tribal Sculpture: Masterpieces from Africa, South East Asia and the Pacific in the Barbier-Mueller Museum* (London, 1995) with H. Waterfield, and *Oceanic Art* (NY, 1997) with A. Kaeppler and C. Kaufmann.

> If we think of the word alone [...], 'Sculpture' projects over our mental screens a dazzling torrent of images [...] which might continue, we feel, endlessly. And behind the consciousness of those images is a subdued awareness...

— and here one can imagine Tippett suggesting a subdued awareness of the presence of archetypes of the collective unconscious. But for Newton it's rather a matter of history. *His* awareness is of 'the thousands of men and women [who] have toiled over the last forty thousand years to create them.' Still, there is the occasional link back from the 1990s to Newton's Tippett phase in the 1940s: for instance to the publication of Layard's *Stone Men of Malekula*. Layard is present behind the section on Vanuatu in *Tribal Sculpture*, with its carvings of hawks that are

> used in the rites when a man was ascending from one grade of rank to a higher one. A great matting kite in a geometric shape resembling the silhouette of a hawk (one of the canoe carvings fixed as its head) was hoisted into the trees for the dances that preceded the final scene.[221]

Shades of one of *The Midsummer Marriage*'s Ritual Dances:

> *The shadow of the Hawk [...] is [...] projected on the stage. [...] The Hawk appears and seems to hover on the cornice of the temple just long enough for the audience to see that it is a girl dancer with a bird mask and huge wings.*

1956, which saw Newton's departure for the U.S.A., was a year after the *Marriage*'s première at Covent Garden. It seems not to be known whether Tippett's Denlein was there to see it, and if he was, whether he was wholly happy with the way its plot had developed. He might possibly have raised an eyebrow at some of the things the composer-librettist had excised from such of their draft-scenes as survived from the original plotting: George/Mark's kissing Strephon, Jack's shape changes (so frequent in earlier draftings but now much reduced and only barely

221 Newton and Waterfield, *Tribal Sculpture*, 19 and 330. Cf. Plate 8.1 above. The last paragraph of *Tribal Sculpture* (p. 346) is *echt* Den Newton in its returning to 'an awareness that the ghosts of unknown centuries are standing behind [the works he has selected for the book]: the human ghosts and the ghosts of their creations that have perished long ago.'

justifying the lines about the 'roles' he has to play), the dialogue between Mme Sosostris and King Fisher, the presentation of the leading couple's 're-humanising' (as Tippett called it) after their transfiguration and the cogent interjection of a chorus-member once they return to reality that Jenifer had connived at the death of her father. Still, one feels that Newton would have been happy that some members at least of the first-night audience were coming to the conclusion that its composer too was 'a great man, indeed'. (After all, he had written in his *Crescendo* essay seven years before that Tippett was 'among the English composers who show most clearly the marks of genius'.)[222] It's not known either whether or not he would have been as happy to find that his own name did not feature in the opera's credits. Tippett had written to him in March 1946 that he had got a great deal out of Newton's 'co-operation in ideas and discussion', going on: 'I must acknowledge that [...] and handsomely as is appropriate'. That might be read as meaning that the composer would one day make a formal public statement of grateful indebtedness, in the first-night programme perhaps. But no; it seems rather to have meant that he was making the statement 'performatively' in the letter itself, and that—in the sort of phrase Tippett was apt to use in emotionally charged situations—That Was That.[223]

In 1991, about 35 years after the première, the composer published his autobiography, *Those Twentieth Century Blues*. There, Newton appears several times in the general whirl of events as one of the 'family': loveable, serviceable, good mind, a bit young for his age perhaps but maturing fast. Yet when the book comes to the genesis of the *Marriage*, the composer simply says, 'I tried to collaborate on the text with Douglas Newton, but we were soon at cross purposes' and promptly changes the subject, declaring elsewhere in the book that he had always been his own librettist for his operas, for all that he had 'occasionally toyed with the notion of a collaboration with a writer or dramatist'.[224] This is very strange. Though the *Aurora Consurgens/Midsummer Marriage* collaboration did break down, it did not do so 'soon' but after all of 30 months;

222 *Crescendo*: see above, n. 150.

223 Cf. 'My father died on Thursday, so that is over': BL292.39 (July 1944); and, *re* Britten's dedicating *Curlew River* to him: 'What an unexpected and extraordinary honour! So that's that.' (Schuttenhelm, *Selected Letters*, 217) 'I must acknowledge...': see n. 134 above.

224 *C20 Blues*, 216 and 51. According to Kemp (*Tippett*, 213), the composer 'gave up [the collaboration on *Marriage*] when it transpired that his material was so personal that the result could only have been a damaging compromise.' Was this Tippett's view in the 1980s or is Kemp putting his own construction on things?

as for being 'at cross purposes', there's next to nothing in the mass of surviving letters from Tippett to Newton to suggest that they were ever seriously at odds. True, Tippett's weighty letter of March 1946 speaks of 'temperamental difficulties', but in its context that seems simply to mean that while the composer was energetic and up-and-go about the project, Newton (never in Tippett's experience a fast worker) had recently been dragging his feet. Why the dismissiveness then? On that, one could take the low road or the high. On the low road, one might speculate that, deep down, Tippett *had* been wounded by Newton's pulling out of the project and that his subconscious had coped with this by fogging his memory of what actually happened between 1943 and 1946, reducing it to nothing more than 'toying'. On the high, one might divine that, well aware as he was of Newton's wide and fast-growing reputation in the 1970s and 1980s as a figure to reckon with in the world of Pacific cultures, the composer thought that it would be tasteless and uncivil to go into detail about their collaboration in the 1940s, as in the end it did fall apart. Since Tippett was a generous and good-natured man, the high road seems more likely to be the right road.

Newton himself, however, didn't want things to rest quite like that. Some years before *Those Twentieth Century Blues*, he had mentioned the idea to Tippett of presenting the British Library with the full sequence of the composer's letters to him. Tippett had been 'coy', 'not charmed', and Newton did nothing. He raised the matter again with their mutual friend John Amis in November 1991 after he had read and relished Amis's *Amiscellany*; but still he let it lie.[225] It was different the following spring when Amis sent him a copy of Tippett's autobiography. He wrote back to say that he had read it and was

> reading it again, with very odd feelings I can't altogether formulate. It's a touching experience and in many ways a very strange one. [...] The bits about me seem weird, naturally so I suppose. I mean that in terms of what appears I can't relate it to myself either as I am now, or as I think I was then. [...] I wish you would advise me about one thing. I mentioned to you years ago that I have kept all of MT's letters, and I'd like to see them safely bestowed. [...] I've thought at times of the British Library. So what do I do with them?[226]

225 Newton to Amis, 30 November 1991; 17–9 January 1996 (quoted by permission, see n. 30 above).

226 Newton to Amis, 11 April 1992 (quoted by permission; see n. 30 above). Late in life, in his unpublished 'Autobiographical Notes', Newton described *C20 Blues* as 'rather chilly' (quoted by permission, see n. 11 above).

Amis took the matter in hand and became the middleman in the letters' eventual lodging at the British Library in 1996. That way, Newton must have felt, a true record of his and Tippett's relationship and the work they did together would enter the public domain. 'I was there,' he seems to be saying, 'and it was like this; people should know.' And we do come to know how involved Newton was at once with the composer's emotional life and with the slow early genesis of a great opera: a genesis revealed in parallel in Tippett's sketchbooks. True, the letters and sketchbooks also tantalise. We want more. Where are Newton's replies? Where is the 1944 scenario for Act I of the *Aurora* masque, where the First Act draft libretto that Newton wrote when masque had become opera? Still, even if these all went into the wastepaper basket 70 years ago, what we do have throws much light on the significant, highly gifted, promising (and later achieving) figure of Douglas Newton, also on Tippett's creative drive and on his singular way of devising an operatic text. He was eloquent after the event about the drive and the devising in his essay of the early 1950s, 'The Birth of an Opera'. As he recalls his first ideas for *Midsummer Marriage*,

> some of the excitement of these first pictures comes back. It is the feeling a creative artist has when he knows he has become the instrument of some collective imaginative experience — or, as Wagner put it, that a myth is coming once more to life. I know that, for me, so soon as this thing starts, I am held willy-nilly and cannot turn back. But I know also that, somewhere or other, in books, in pictures, in dreams, in real situations, everything is sooner or later to be found which *belongs* for all the details of the work, which is, as it were, ordained. And everything is accepted or rejected eventually according to whether it *fits* this preordained *thing*, which itself will not be fully known until it is finished.[227]

Reading the letters and sketchbooks of the 1940s brings us close to these mental states and to that fertile jumble of books, pictures, dreams, situations: also to the intransigent determination that gripped Tippett when possessed by the 'myth' to which he felt he had to give new expression—an intransigence that could sit uneasily with his need for warm human companionship—and to the singular amalgam of fixity and freewheeling flexibility that marked his shaping of the myth. Crosswords into crystal bowls, toothed fish into stooping hawks, mandorlas into mandalas: change, given its head, will lead to permanence.

227 Bowen, *Tippett on Music*, 201.

Appendix I
Four poems by Douglas Newton

1. Archaic art

Black panes enframe the life of man:
These Attic vases raise in me
The awe with which the childless see
The ancient games that children play.

A satyr grips his springing tail.
Siamese twins, two horsemen ride:
A raven's knitted to a crop,
A limber rabbit trots beside.

An agile dog beseeches knees
And shins of Master; Father holds
A horse which snuffs a poppy flower
Tarnishing in Mother's hand.

Or grieving Ajax underneath a palm
Kneels to prepare the acrid blade
(His armour, like an armoured ghost,
Looks on, and does not say a word).

A mother mourns her loss among the trees,
But we are strangely consoled, at the turn of a hand:
Look, her neighbours! a man,
Quivering stiff with excitement, grips a girl.

I fear the tranquil marble youths —
Calves on their nape like garlands ride —

Who smile because they know the truth
Whose beauty blinded Oedipus.

How shall I face the girls of stone?
Who stare me down in every dream,
Upon whose loins pleats ripple like
The pebbled waters of a stream.

Hearing your footsteps on the stair
I've know my room reel north to south
Tremendous virgin! — on whose mouth
Gutters the dead-Medusa smile.

2. Bishop and naturalist, 1698–1764

Pontoppidan was walking on the sand,
his cassock gripped by wind against his knee;
and as he watched the frothy dark blue waves
he heard the sailors singing out at sea.
And in a notebook held in his left hand
sighing he wrote the stories they had told:
and they were ignorant, and they were slaves:
but he'd not hear the mermaid rap the side
or see the kraken's vomit stain the tide.

3. Rose and compass

Lo, here's a darling of the earth!
Lovers of roses and of girls
Value a single bloom above
Pearls culled from Cleopatra's ears.

So, Captain, clasp with all the power
Within your hand the guiding thorn.
The wind-rose is the only flower
Borne by the salt champagnes of sea.

4. A death-mask

We stare into the case
At Agamemnon's mask,
The crinkled golden face
That gleams below the glass
An underwater carp
Dormant in its pool:
I wonder as I look
How grains of earth should feel
Condensed upon its cold;
And stifled from the sight
Through the dark thousand years
In what immortal light
Did those great eyelids shine?

Appendix II
Newton, bibliography to 1956

I. Published work

1942 *The Fortune Anthology* (Fortune Press), edited by Douglas Newton, Nicholas Moore and John Bayliss; includes 'From the Editors' (by all three of them) and a review by DN of Osbert Sitwell, *Open the Door!* (pp. 69–74).

1942–43 Film reviews in *The Cambridge Review*, e.g. 64 (1942–43), 105, 168, 216, 301–2; 65 (1943–44), 60, 95, 134.

1944 Two poems—'Songes and Sonettes' and 'A Face like the Sun' [both written 1943]—in *New Poetry* (ed. N. Moore), I, 1 and 4.

1945 *Atlantic Anthology* (Fortune Press), edited by DN and N. Moore, inc. three poems (pp. 4–5) by DN: 'A Death-Mask' [1944], 'Shuttle-Cock' [1945], 'Lacking a Guide' [1944].

'The Artist's Responsibility' [essay], *New English Weekly*, 28/3 (1.xi.45), 25–6.

1946 'The Character of Creon' [on the Old Vic *Oedipus*], *New English Weekly*, 28/13 (10.i.46).

'Five Poems by Douglas Newton': 'Cherubs of Venus' [1945], 'Bishop and Naturalist, 1698–1764' [1942], 'Gaiety of Descendants: A Sailor's Song' [1945], 'Archaic Art' [1944], 'Night Piece' [1944] — in *Poetry (Chicago)*, 68/3 (June 1946), 130–3.

'A Note on Henry Miller', *New English Weekly*, 30/10 (19. xii.46), 98–9.

1947 'Invasion Weather' [1944], *The Penguin New Writing*, No. 29, 92.

'Onionskin Man' [1946], *Poetry (Chicago)*, 70/5 (August 1947), 243.

'The Annunciation to the Virgin Mary' [1947]: pamphlet publication by Anthony Froshaug (run of 100 copies).

'Paul Goodman and "Scientific Expressionism" ': review of Paul Goodman, *The Facts of Life*, *New English Weekly*, 31/3 (1.v.47), 27.

1948 'Disguises of the Artist' [1944], *The Penguin New Writing*, No. 33, 94.

'Michael Tippett' [essay], *Crescendo*, 14 (March 1948), 5–7 and 13.

'Sport in Art', *Future*, 3/4 (1948), 63ff.

1949 'The Composer and the Music of Poetry', *The Score*, I/1, 13–20.

'The Fragments of Orpheus' [postcard poem].

1950 'In Saint Anthony's Harbour', *Poetry (London)*, 5/18, 19–21.

1951 'The Sea and Mr Auden' [review of W. H. Auden, *The Enchafèd Flood*], *Poetry (London)*, 6 (Winter 1951), 30.

Catalogue for '*Black Eyes and Lemonade*: A Festival of Britain Exhibition of British Popular and Traditional Art', organised by Barbara Jones and Tom Ingram, Whitechapel Gallery.

1951–54 Brief illustrated articles for *Far and Wide* (Guest Keen and Nettlefold Group), e.g. 'The Cactus in Modern Decoration' (Summer 1951, 38–41), 'Children's Games' (Winter 1951–52, 32–6), 'The Science of Equitation' (Winter 1953–54, 12–15).

1952 Short illustrated pieces for *The Architectural Review*, 111, 191–5 ('Printed Textiles'); 112, 55–7 ('Terence Conran at Simpson's').

Metamorphoses of Violence: Crescendo Poetry Series No.7 (The Latin Press, St Ives). Dedicated to Mary Lee Settle. This collects five of the earlier published poems and adds four new ones: 'An Emblem', 'Love and Wars of Mars and Venus' [1946], 'Marshfield' [1947] and 'Landscapes of Night and Day' — the last being later reprinted in *Paris Review*, Spring 1954, 122–3. ('The Annunciation to the Virgin Mary' is reprinted here with the added dedication: 'In Honour of Claudio Monteverdi'.)

1952–1956 Book-reviews (quite brief in the main) for *Time and Tide*, Vols. 33–7: nine in 1952, seven in 1953, seven in 1954, five in 1955 and one in 1956.

1953 'Rebus: or The Poet's Education', dedicated to Edric Maynard, *Botteghe Oscure*, 11, 141–51.

'The Leaves of Life', *Time and Tide*, 34, 372.

1954 'Foundations of Our City', *Botteghe Oscure*, 13, 146–9.

1955 'Lights with Us: A Dialogue', *Botteghe Oscure*, 15, 163–99.

1956 *Hymns as Poetry*, anthology compiled by DN and Tom Ingram (Constable). Dedicated to Mary Lee Settle and Barbara Jones.

II. Unpublished poems

Letters of Michael Tippett's and Edith Sitwell's refer to other poems from the 1940s that seem not to have made print, among them 'News Item', 'Friends', 'Kinds of Spice' and 'Memorial Sequence'. Further, in that decade DN planned and assembled a collection (unpublished, surviving as a cuttings-book in his Archive) which was to be called *Love and Mythology* and which would have been dedicated to Francesca Allinson. Along with 16 poems either already published or soon to be so, the cuttings-book includes the following seemingly unpublished ones, all dated by Newton on the contents page: 'Green Street' [1942], 'Rose and Compass' [1944], 'The Warm Statues' [1943], 'Constellations' [1945], 'Getting Acquainted' [1943], 'Obscure Games' [1945], 'An Era's Glass' [1945], 'In Autumn' [1946], 'Descent of the Lord' [1945], 'Nature Morte' [1944], 'The Blind Children' [1946], 'And on His Shoulder' [1947], 'The End of Potymkin' [1943, '47]. (The dates assigned in square brackets to individual poems in the yearly entries from 1944 to 1948 in Part I of this Bibliography above also derive from this contents-page.) Cuttings-book, in Box 5 of The Douglas Newton Archive © 2017 Virginia-Lee Webb PhD; All Rights Reserved. Cited by permission.

Appendix III
Tippett, The British Library sketchbooks

Here follows an informal inventory of the material connected with scenarios, scripts and librettos in these six exercise books (Add. MSS 72054-9). Almost all the material listed is to be found by reading the books front-to-back in the usual way. If one turns them upside down and reads as-it-were back to front, one finds quite copious MS material for radio talks, essays, etc., largely unconnected directly with the making of *Aurora Consurgens* or *The Midsummer Marriage*. With two exceptions, I have not included any of the 'upside-down' material in the following.

First Sketchbook: 72054

2r: The 'Octett' trigram-octagon from the *I Ching* (with four Element-Instrument parallels), as reproduced in *C20 Blues*, 215.

2v-3r: Draft title-page for libretto + Foreword (1944?) (see above pp. 55–6), plus postscript to Foreword (1946?) (see above p. 77).

4r: The four remaining Element-Instrument parallels, and an epigraph: ' "We have lost the up-and-down dimension in existence": V. A. Demant, "The Challenge of Our Time" BBC talk: 1st week of May 46.' (The talk, on the BBC Home Service, was by the Anglo-Catholic Rev. Vigo Auguste Demant, 1893–1983, and was printed in *The Listener*, 9 May 1946, pp. 599–600, as 'The Fairy Ring of Civilisation: V. A. Demant on "The Challenge of Our Time" ': 'We have lost the up-and-down dimension of existence — the penetration of eternity into time — the spiritual depth in all finite things that can give meaning to the temporal process.')

4v-9v: Roughed-out dialogue (to be sung and spoken) plus stage-directions in 'script'-form (quite early in date?), from the entrance of the Neophytes to George's 'I go to hell: I'll teach her!' Includes the Neophyte choir's welcome to the Ancients (see above, pp. 60–1), Jack's entry in his plumber's overalls (for all that he is supposed to be acting as George's Best Man), plus Margaret entering 'in mountaineering costume' and later performing a ritualised 'strip-teaze' ('Recitative, Scena and Ensemble') as she mounts the steps. ('Naked I stand in the heavenly light.')

10r: Draft fragment of the George-Margaret *agon* in Act I.

10v: Draft sequence, from Sosostris asking for the magic bowl to Strephon's joining the action. 'The snake (or fish) Crab Octopus Strephon to the rescue. The net'

Second Sketchbook: 72055

2r-2v: Draft scenario for Act II Sc. 1 of the Masque (the 'Windrose' scene) and Sc. 2; *circa* Feb 1944 (see transcript above, pp. 38–9).

3r: Table of musical keys as they relate to plot-episodes in a version of the planned Act I. See p. 61, n. 130 above, n.130 above.

3v-12r: The rest of the Act II draft scenario, *circa* Feb 1944 (see transcript above, pp. 39–47), with 6v containing further notes on keys.

12v-71v + 75v-76r: Sketches, drafts and try-outs, largely (perhaps wholly) from summer 1946 and after, including:

13r-21r: Elaborate plans for the Jack-at-the-Gates ensemble.

22v: Margaret becomes Jenifer, or rather 'Jennifer' in the first instance (= late 1940s); characterisations of semi-transfigured hero and heroine (see above, p. 52–3).

35v: George's evoking his love for Margaret-Jenifer in his account of his 'hell' visit ('Still the image of my lover / Drew me on yet barred me not').

45v-46v: Script-notes for the 'new' Act II, *post*-Newton but *pre*-E. W. White's creative intervention. Scenes 1 and 2: *four* Ritual Dances/Race Dances followed by Bella's entry:

[...] Strephon with a certain submissive air joins the young men who group around him, shutting him from view. The girls form a complementary group. When the groups break up soon after[,] Strephon has become a hare, while one (or more) of the girls has become a greyhound bitch. The scene is thus set for the

First Race Dance
Strephon runs 'home' first and is received into the men's group again. This time he is changed into a fish, the girl into a bitch-otter. Then follows the

Second Race-dance
Strephon swims 'home' first. The third changes are into a bird and a hawk. Follows the

Third Race-dance
Strephon flies ('home') to safety. The fourth changes are into an ear/a sheaf of corn and a crested hen. Follows the

Fourth Race-dance
Strephon, who has reached safety with increasing difficulty, might even reach home safely a fourth and last time did not one of the young men cut him down with a sickle. As the hen poises to peck the corn-ear Bella is heard singing off. There is a moment of immobility before the dancers vanish back into the trees as Bella enters. Strephon picks up his corn-sheaf and runs off into the temple.

Sc 2 Bella (off): (Life's dull until the work is over)
Entering L) When you and I walk out to —
She drops her handbag and turns back to the wings.
Jack, Jack come quickly.
Hurry please I want you.
Jack (enters) I stopped to pick a flower for you.
(clinging to him) Thank heaven you're here.
You're all a tremble.
What is the matter?
I saw the dancers [...]
[It is the apparent metamorphosis of the dancers into trees that has upset Bella.]

56r-v, 65v-66v: Notes for a version of the Messenger / Telegraph-Boy Scene, on which see White, *Tippett*, 54; and a further version of the dance-scene with Bella interrupting the attack on the bird by the 'hawk (or falcon)'; *circa* Sept 1949.

70r-71r: A transitional version—George becomes Lance (Tippett was 'toying' with this name in November 1949: White, *Tippett*, 59–60)—of the finale to Act III with the Yeats quotation in place, followed by a terminal 'Shantih!?'

85r to 84v (i.e. upside down): Notes for final scene, including a reviving of the crumpled King Fisher involving the He-Ancient and Strephon.

Third Sketchbook: 72056

A sequence of drafts for lines in the opera, seemingly set down at the transitional point where the old masque-scenario with Neophyte chorus (plus Magic Net, Fish, Barrel and a Finale involving both pairs of mortal lovers) is still in operation but is giving way to a new scenario that involves a chorus of George and Margaret's wedding guests. There are many lines which survive into the final 1952 text, including 'Sirius rising…' and 'Was it a vision? Was it a dream?', but some interesting ones that do not, including:

'We are th'eternal spectators …' etc. (see above, p. 78).

George to the Ancients: 'It's spring: I cannot stop it', which is scored out and replaced by 'It's Midsummer morn and anything can happen'.

George of Strephon: 'He dances his answers to my words...'

King Fisher to Jack: 'Take the belt and holster / Symbol of the state's authority', at which 'Strephon dances in anguish around Jack'.

'Children, unhang the magic net…' (see above, p. 81).

'Pride undid him…' (see above, p. 79).

'Now the weddings can take place at last…' [plus the She-Ancient's pitcher of wine] (see above, p. 79).

There are also, beyond the major removal of the Barrel intrigue, some plot-moments in these drafts that don't survive into the finished opera, including:

Jack being late for the wedding at which he's to be Best Man because he's doing a plumbing job for Bella's mother (as also in First Sketchbook);

The Voice Behind the Gates being not Sosostris but 'Choir (off), Men?';

Bella's glimpsing Strephon's Girl for a moment, and the Faun's turning to stone (see above, p. 49–50);

King Fisher and Sosostris exchanging several lines of dialogue, Greek-tragedy-style, which involve Sosostris being made to look more than once into the bowl and her seeing King Fisher dead there (so provoking his 'It's all a hoax, a sham').

Fourth Sketchbook: 72057

1r-7r only: libretto sketches, mainly King Fisher's harangue to the Chorus Boys in Act I.

Fifth Sketchbook: 72058

Notable for two things —

a 5v-18r: Extensive rough notes for an *I Ching*-based 'family'-project (see above, p. 20).

b 91v-85v (*sic*, i.e. upside-down): plot-summary by MT of the completed *Midsummer Marriage*.

Sixth Sketchbook: 72059

1v-49v: Up to 42r there is a fairly continuous draft of Act III, plus numerous tryings-out of phrases for it: probably from 1950–51, since the 'royal pair' are now Mark and Jenifer and very little happens that isn't paralleled in the final 1952 text, though King Fisher briefly has a personal name; Sosostris has yet to be given her lines from Valéry;

Sosostris and King Fisher have a heated exchange; Mark and Jenifer incandesce with Strephon in something closer to an almond (a *mandorla*) than a lotus—see p. 82 above—and at the very end Strephon summons *both* pairs of lovers for a coming-together quartet (see p. 79 above). 42v-49v are rather more miscellaneous, including Jenifer's mixed feelings about the death of her father.

Re King Fisher's name: in a second version of the eventually dropped scene with the Telegraph Boy's delivery (2r), King Fisher signs his telegram to Jack and Bella 'Amangons'. (MT says early in 1950 that he found this name for the actual Fisher King who had laid the Waste Land waste in a 'source on Druidism' [White, *Tippett*, 61–2]—presumably L. Spence, *History and Origins of Druidism* [London, 1949], 137–8—though it was there to be found in Weston's

From Ritual to Romance, 172–3.) *Re* Sosostris: before acquiring her lines from Valéry she was to sing instead:

> When once I look within the bowl,
> I lose all knowledge of myself.
> My womanhood, rich, shadowed self
> Dissolves into a greater self
> To wake an instrument [...]

Select Bibliography

Studies etc. since 1940

(Place of books' publication London unless otherwise indicated)

Amis, John, *Amiscellany: My Life, My Music* (1985)
Bowen, Meirion, *Michael Tippett*, 2nd ed. (1997)
Cairns, David, *Responses: Musical Essays and Reviews* (1963), 33–45
Carnegy, Patrick, 'The Composer as Librettist', *TLS* (8 July 1977), 834–5
Clarke, David, *The Music and Thought of Michael Tippett: Modern Times and Metaphysics* (Cambridge, 2001)
Davies, J. L., '"A Visionary Night"', in N. John, ed., *The Operas of Michael Tippett* (ENO Opera Guide 29: 1985), 53–62
Duncan, Ronald, *How to Make Enemies* (1968)
Eliot, T. S., *The Poems of T. S. Eliot*, ed. C. Ricks and J. McCue (2015)
Graves, Robert, *The White Goddess: A Historical Grammar of Poetic Myth* (1948)
Jones, R. E., *The Early Operas of Michael Tippett* (Lewiston, 1996)
Jung, C. G., *The Essential Jung: Selected Writings*, ed. A. Storr (Princeton, 1983)
———, *The Integration of the Personality*, tr. S. Dell (1940)
———, *Memories, Dreams, Reflections*, ed. A. Jaffé (1947)
———, *Psychological Types* (*Collected Works*, Vol. 6, tr. H. Baynes and R. Hull: 1971)
———, *The Symbolic Life* (*Collected Works*, Vol. 18, tr. R. Hull: 1976)
Kemp, Ian, ed., *Michael Tippett: A Symposium on His 60th Birthday* (1965)
———, *Tippett: The Composer and His Music* (1984)
Kjellgren, Eric, 'Returning to the Source: Michael C. Rockefeller, Douglas Newton, and the Arts of Oceania', *The Metropolitan Museum of Art Bulletin*, Summer (2014), 28–37
Layard, John, *The Lady of the Hare* (1944)
———, *Stone Men of Malekula: Vao* (1942)
Levy, Gertrude, *The Gate of Horn* (1948)
Lewis, Geraint, ed., *Michael Tippett O.M.: A Celebration* (Tunbridge Wells, 1985)

Mattet, Laurence, 'Entretien avec Douglas Newton', *Arts & Cultures*, 1 (2000), 19–30

Newton, Douglas: see Appendix II above

Porter, Andrew '*The Midsummer Marriage*', *Opera* 6 (Feb 1955), 77–82

Robinson, Suzanne, ed., *Michael Tippett: Music and Literature* (Aldershot, 2002)

Savage, Robert, 'On Truth and Semblance in an Operatic and Extra-Operatic Sense: Michael Tippett's *The Midsummer Marriage*', *Opera Quarterly* 25 (2009), 270–83

Settle, M. L., *All the Brave Promises* (Columbia SC, 1995)

———, *Learning to Fly: A Writer's Memoir*, ed. A. Freeman (New York, 2007)

Soden, Oliver, *Michael Tippett: The Biography* (2019)

Southworth, Helen, *Fresca: A Life in the Making* (Brighton, 2017)

Stanford, Derek, *Christopher Fry Album* (1952)

———, *Inside the Forties* (1977)

Tippett, Michael, *Moving into Aquarius* (1959)

———, *Selected Letters of Michael Tippett*, ed. T. Schuttenhelm (2005)

———, *Those Twentieth Century Blues: An Autobiography* (1991)

———, *Tippett on Music*, ed. M. Bowen (Oxford, 1995)

Webb. V.-L., 'Douglas Newton (1920–2001)', *Pacific Arts* (July 2001), 171–2

White, E. W., *Tippett and His Operas* (1979)

Whittall, Arnold, *The Music of Britten and Tippett* (Cambridge, 1982)

Wilhelm, Richard, *The I Ching or Book of Changes*, tr. C. Baynes, 3rd ed. (1968)

Zimmer, Heinrich, *Myths and Symbols in Indian Art and Civilisation* (Washington, DC, 1946)

Index

Note: Page numbers followed by "n" denote footnotes